Ready Notes
Volume II, Chapters 13-26

for use with

FUNDAMENTAL ACCOUNTING PRINCIPLES

Fifteenth Edition

Kermit D. Larson
University of Texas at Austin, Emeritus

John J. Wild
University of Wisconsin at Madison

Barbara Chiappetta
Nassau Community College

Prepared by
Jon A. Booker
Charles W. Caldwell
Susan C. Galbreath
Richard S. Rand
All of Tennessee Technological University

Irwin
McGraw-Hill

Boston Burr Ridge, IL Dubuque, IA Madison, WI New York San Francisco St. Louis
Bangkok Bogotá Caracas Lisbon London Madrid
Mexico City Milan New Delhi Seoul Singapore Sydney Taipei Toronto

Irwin/McGraw-Hill

*A Division of The **McGraw-Hill** Companies*

Ready Notes, Volume II, Chapters 13-26, for use with
FUNDAMENTAL ACCOUNTING PRINCIPLES

2 3 4 5 6 7 8 9 0 BKM/BKM 9 3 2 1 0 9

ISBN 0-07-030589-7

http://www.mhhe.com

Welcome to

READY NOTES

Your life just got easier! This booklet includes *Ready Notes* to accompany your textbook. *Ready Notes* were designed as a classroom supplement to accompany *Ready Shows*. More importantly, *Ready Notes* were developed for you, the student.

Somewhere in your educational experience, you have undoubtedly encountered a common dilemma facing many students; the feeling of helplessness that comes from trying to write down everything your instructor says and, at the same time, actually paying attention to what is being taught. *Ready Notes* addresses this problem by providing pre-prepared lecture outlines to accompany the *Ready Shows* your instructor will be using in class. Rather than spending time copying material that is already in the book, you will be able to focus on the most important aspects of what your instructor is actually saying. You will still be expected to take notes, but the nature of those notes will change.

Each page in *Ready Notes* includes reproductions of some of the actual projected screens that you will be seeing in class. The *Ready Notes* booklet includes the information for many of the examples that your instructor will be presenting.

It is your responsibility to attend class regularly and to be prepared for class. However, used properly, Ready Notes will help you to achieve your goals for the course. Good luck and good accounting!

CONTENTS

13 CHAPTER Partnerships and Corporations

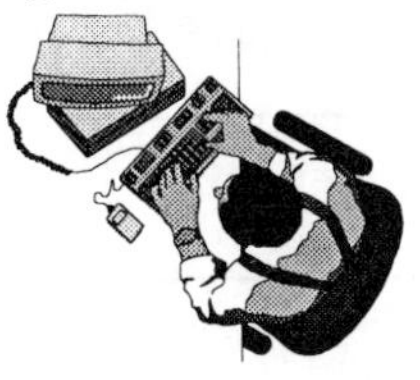

Characteristics of Partnerships

- Voluntary Association
- Partnership Agreement
- Limited Life
- Taxation
- Mutual Agency
- Unlimited Liability
- Co-Ownership of Property

Limited Partnerships

Two classes of partners:

General Partners	Limited Partners
Management has responsibilities & liability is unlimited.	Liability is limited to the amount of the investment

Limited Liability Partnerships (L.L.P.)

L.L.P.'s are designed to protect innocent partners from malpractice or negligence of other partners.

All partners still have unlimited liability for partnership debts.

Organizing a Partnership

When partners invest in a partnership, their capital accounts are credited for the fair value of their invested amounts.

On January 11, 1999, Steeley and Breck organize the partnership called BOARDS. Steeley invests $7,000 cash, $33,000 in boarding facilities, and a $10,000 note payable. Breck invests $10,000 cash.

Prepare the entries to record each partner's investment.

Organizing a Partnership

Remember: Steeley invested $7,000 cash, $33,000 in boarding facilities, and a $10,000 note payable.

GENERAL JOURNAL — Page 1

Date		Description	PR	Debit	Credit

Organizing a Partnership

Breck invested $10,000 cash in BOARDS.

GENERAL JOURNAL					Page 1
Date		Description	PR	Debit	Credit

Additional Partnership Accounts

Net income

Additional capital contributions

Increases

Partners' Capital Balances

Decreases

Net loss

Capital withdrawals

Division of Earnings

In absence of an agreement stating otherwise, partnership income or loss is shared equally by the partners.

Division of Earnings

Possible ways to divide partnership earnings:

- Use a stated fractional basis.
- Use the ratio of capital investments.
- Use salary and interest allowances with any remainder of earnings divided according to a fixed ratio.

Irwin/McGraw-Hill

Earnings Allocated on a Stated Fractional Basis

Steeley and Breck agree to divide partnership earnings in the ratio of two-thirds to Steeley and one-third to Breck.

If BOARDS earns $60,000 in 2001, how much net income will be allocated to each partner?

GENERAL JOURNAL — **Page 1**

Date		Description	PR	Debit	Credit

Irwin/McGraw-Hill

Allocating Using Salaries, Interest and a Fixed Ratio

If partner service or capital contributions are not equal, salary and interest allowances can compensate for the differences.

Irwin/McGraw-Hill

Allocating Using Salaries, Interest and a Fixed Ratio

Example: Browne and Greene agree on salary allowances of $30,000 and $20,000, respectively. Browne invested $25,000 in the partnership and Greene invested $50,000.

Each partner receives 10 percent interest on capital invested. Any remaining income after allowances is divided equally.

If partnership income is $90,000, how much does each partner receive?

Allocating Using Salaries, Interest and a Fixed Ratio

Example continued: The partnership income was sufficient to cover salary and interest allowances. Now assume that partnership income is only $40,000, but all other information remains the same. How much does each partner receive?

Purchase of Partnership Interest

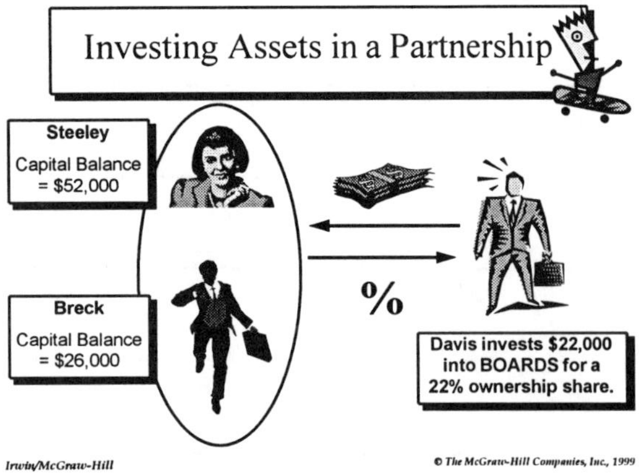
Investing Assets in a Partnership
Steeley
Capital Balance = $52,000
Breck
Capital Balance = $26,000
%
Davis invests $22,000 into BOARDS for a 22% ownership share.
Irwin/McGraw-Hill
© The McGraw-Hill Companies, Inc., 1999

Bonus to Old Partners
Steeley
Capital Balance = $52,000
Breck
Capital Balance = $26,000
25 %
Davis invests $42,000 into BOARDS for a 25% ownership share.
Irwin/McGraw-Hill
© The McGraw-Hill Companies, Inc., 1999

Bonus to New Partner
When a new partner brings special skills or expertise to the partnership, the existing partners will often pay a “bonus” to the new partner.
The new partner is then credited with a capital balance that exceeds his cash contribution.
Davis invests in BOARDS for a 25% ownership share. He also is a world champion skate boarder.
Irwin/McGraw-Hill
© The McGraw-Hill Companies, Inc., 1999

Withdrawal of a Partner - No Bonus

Steeley
Capital Balance = $84,000

Breck
Capital Balance = $38,000

Breck withdraws from the partnership and receives cash equal to his capital balance.

Davis
Capital Balance = $38,000

Withdrawal of a Partner - Other Situations

Bonus to Remaining Partners	**Bonus to Withdrawing Partner**
• Withdrawing partner receives cash **less** than current capital balance. • The difference is **added** to remaining partners' accounts.	• Withdrawing partner receives cash **greater** than current capital balance. • The difference is **subtracted** from remaining partners' accounts.

Characteristics of Corporations

An entity created by law.

Existence is separate from owners.

Has rights and privileges.

Ownership can be

Privately Held

Publicly Held

Choosing A Business Form

	Proprietorship	Partnership	LLP	Corporation
Business Entity	Yes	Yes	Yes	Yes
Legal Entity	No	No	No	Yes
Limited Liability	No	No	Limited	Yes
Business Taxed	No	No	No	Yes
One Owner Allowed	Yes	No	No	Yes

Management of a Corporation

Corporate Organization Chart

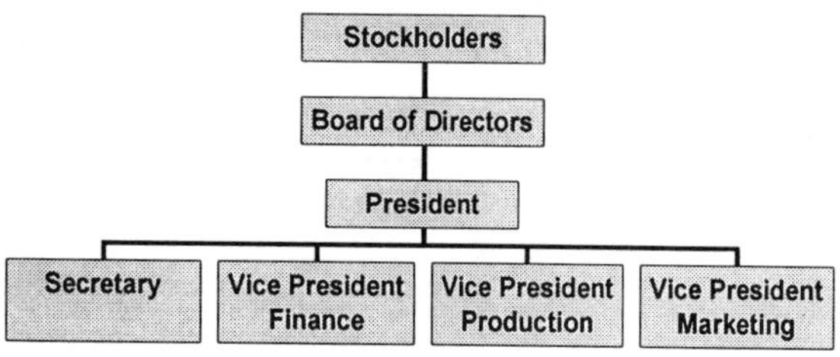

Rights of Stockholders

❶ Vote at stockholders' meetings.
❷ Sell stock.
❸ Purchase additional shares of stock.
❹ Share equally with other common stockholders in any dividends.
❺ Share equally in any assets remaining after creditors are paid in a liquidation of corporate assets.

Stock Certificates and Transfer

Each unit of ownership is called a share of stock.

A stock certificate serves as proof that a stockholder has purchased shares.

Selling Stock

Par value is an arbitrary amount assigned to each share of stock when it is authorized.

Market price is the amount that each share of stock will sell for in the market.

Common Stock

Common stock can be issued in three forms:

- Par Value Common Stock
- No Par Common Stock
- Stated Value Common Stock

Let's examine this form of stock (Par Value Common Stock)

Issuing Par Value Stock

Par Value Stock

Prepare the journal entry to record an issuance of 10,000 shares of $20 par value stock for $25 per share which occurred on September 1, 1999.

Record:

The cash received.

The number of shares issued × the par value per share in the Common Stock account.

The remainder is assigned to Contributed Capital in Excess of Par.

Issuing Par Value Stock

Par Value Stock

Prepare the journal entry to record an issuance of 10,000 shares of $20 par value stock for $25 per share which occurred on September 1, 1999.

GENERAL JOURNAL — Page 1

Date		Description	PR	Debit	Credit

Exh. 13.6

Stockholders' Equity

Proprietorship	Partnership	Corporation
C. Taylor, Capital (Normal, bal.)	C. Taylor, Capital (Normal, bal.)	Common Stock (Normal, bal.)
	J. Taylor, Capital (Normal, bal.)	Contributed Capital in Excess of Par (Normal, bal.)
		Retained Earnings (Normal, bal.)

Preferred Stock

A separate class of stock, typically having priority over common shares in . . .

- Dividend distributions.
- Distribution of assets in case of liquidation.

Usually has a stated dividend rate.

Normally has no voting rights.

Preferred Stock

Cumulative Vs. Noncumulative

Cumulative: Dividends in arrears must be paid before dividends may be paid on common stock.

Noncumulative: Undeclared dividends from current and prior years do not have be paid in future years.

Allocation of Preferred Dividends

Example: Consider the following partial Statement of Stockholders' Equity

Common stock, $50 par value; 4,000 shares authorized, issued and outstanding	$ 200,000
Preferred stock, 9%, $100 par value; 1,000 shares authorized, issued and outstanding	100,000
Total contributed capital	$ 300,000

During 1999, the directors declare cash dividends of $5,000. In year 2000, the directors declare cash dividends of $42,000.

14 CHAPTER Corporate Financial Reporting

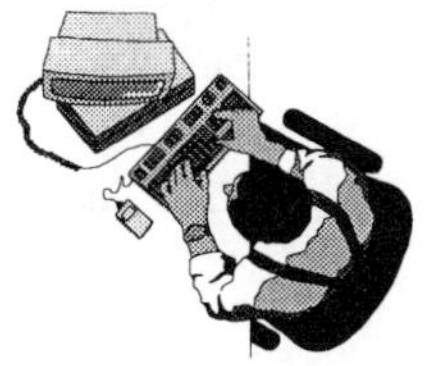

Dividends

To pay a cash dividend the corporation must have a sufficient balance in retained earnings and the cash necessary to pay the dividend.

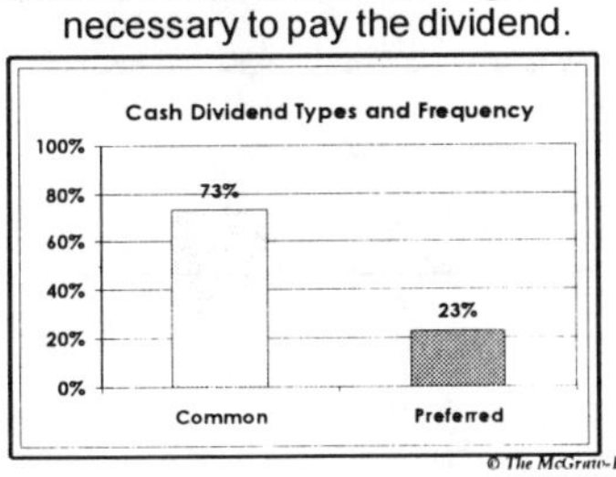

Dividends

Regular cash dividends provide a return to investors and almost always affect the stock's market value.

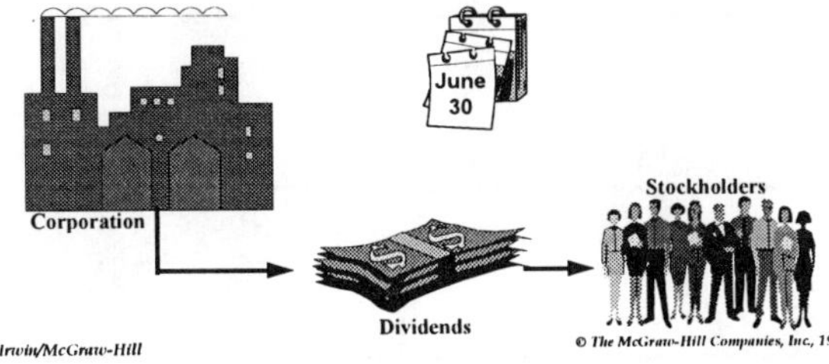

Entries for Cash Dividends

Three important dates

Date of Declaration	Date of Record	Date of Payment
Record liability for dividend.	No entry required.	Record payment of cash to stockholders.

Entries for Cash Dividends

On January 19, a $1 per share cash dividend is declared on Dana, Inc.'s 10,000 common shares outstanding.

GENERAL JOURNAL — Page 4

Date		Description	PR	Debit	Credit
Jan	19				

Date of Declaration

Record liability for dividend.

Entries for Cash Dividends

On January 19, a $1 per share cash dividend is declared on Dana, Inc.'s 10,000 common shares outstanding. The date of record is February 19.

GENERAL JOURNAL — Page 34

Date		Description	PR	Debit	Credit
Feb	19	No Entry Required			

Date of Record

No entry required.

Entries for Cash Dividends

On January 19, a $1 per share cash dividend is declared on Dana, Inc.'s 10,000 common shares outstanding. The date of record is February 19. The dividend is paid on March 19.

Date of Payment

Record payment of cash to stockholders.

GENERAL JOURNAL — Page 78

Date		Description	PR	Debit	Credit
Mar	19				

Stockholders' Equity with a Deficit

Created when a company incurs cumulative losses or pays dividends greater than total profits earned in other years.

Dana, Inc.
Stockholders' Equity
December 31, 1999

Stockholders' Equity	
Common stock $10 par value,	
10,000 shares authorized and outstanding	$ 100,000
Retained earnings deficit	(8,500)
Total stockholders' equity	$ 91,500

Liquidating Cash Dividends

A liquidating cash dividend occurs in some states that allow cash dividends to be paid as a return on the capital contributed by stockholders.

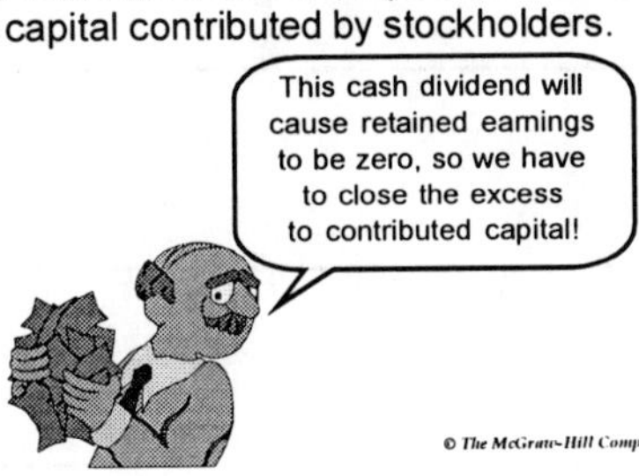

Stock Dividends

The corporation distributes additional shares of its own stock to its stockholders without receiving any payment in return.

Stock Dividends

The corporation distributes additional shares of its own stock to its stockholders without receiving any payment in return.

Why a stock dividend?

Can be used to keep the market price on the stock affordable.

Can provide evidence of management's confidence that the company is doing well.

Entries for Stock Dividend

<u>Small Stock Dividend</u>

- Distribution is ≤ 25% of the previously outstanding shares.
- Capitalize retained earnings for the market value of the shares to be distributed.

<u>Large Stock Dividend</u>

- Distribution is > 25% of the previously outstanding shares.
- Capitalize retained earnings for the minimum amount required by state law, usually par or stated value of the shares.

Entries for Stock Dividend

Exh. 14-2

Here is the stockholders' equity section of X-Quest's balance sheet prior to the declaration of a stock dividend.

X-Quest Stockholders' Equity December 31, 2000	
Common stock - $10 par value, 15,000 shares authorized, 10,000 shares issued and outstanding	$ 100,000
Contributed capital in excess of par value	8,000
Total contributed capital	$ 108,000
Retained earnings	35,000
Total stockholders' equity	$ 143,000

Recording a Small Stock Dividend

On December 31, 2000, X-Quest declared a 10% stock dividend, when the stock was selling for $15 per share. The stock will be distributed to stockholders on January 20, 2001. Let's make the December 31 entry.

GENERAL JOURNAL — Page 13

Date		Description	PR	Debit	Credit
Dec	31				

Recording a Small Stock Dividend

The Stock Dividend Declared account is closed to Retained Earnings with the following entry.

GENERAL JOURNAL — Page 13

Date		Description	PR	Debit	Credit
Dec	31	Retained Earnings		15,000	
		Stock Dividend Declared			15,000

Recording a Small Stock Dividend

Exh. 14-3

The stockholders' equity of X-Quest's balance sheet on December 31, 2000, now looks like this.

X-Quest Stockholders' Equity December 31, 2000	
Common stock - $10 par value,	
15,000 shares authorized,	
10,000 shares issued and outstanding	$ 100,000
Common stock distributable, 100 shares	10,000
Total common stock issued and to be issued	$ 110,000
Contributed capital in excess of par value	13,000
Total contributed capital	$ 123,000
Retained earnings	20,000
Total stockholders' equity	$ 143,000

Recording a Small Stock Dividend

On January 20, 2001, the shares of stock are issued to our stockholders. Let's prepare the necessary entry.

GENERAL JOURNAL Page 13

Date		Description	PR	Debit	Credit
Jan	20				

Before the stock dividend.

X-Quest Stockholders' Equity December 31, 2000	
Common stock - $10 par value,	
15,000 shares authorized,	
10,000 shares issued and outstanding	$ 100,000
Contributed capital in excess of par value	8,000
Total contributed capital	$ 108,000
Retained earnings	35,000
Total stockholders' equity	$ 143,000

After the stock dividend.

X-Quest Stockholders' Equity January 20, 2001	
Common stock - $10 par value,	
15,000 shares authorized,	
11,000 shares issued and outstanding	$110,000
Contributed capital in excess of par value	13,000
Total contributed capital	$123,000
Retained earnings	20,000
Total stockholders' equity	$143,000

Recording a Large Stock Dividend

Rounder, Inc. shows the following stockholders' equity section just prior to issuing a large stock dividend.

Rounder, Inc. Stockholders' Equity December 31, 1999	
Common stock - $1 par value, 100,000 shares authorized, 50,000 shares issued and outstanding	$ 50,000
Contributed capital in excess of par value	75,000
Total contributed capital	125,000
Retained earnings	100,000
Total stockholders' equity	$ 225,000

Recording a Large Stock Dividend

On December 31, 1999, Rounder declared a 40% stock dividend, when the stock was selling for $8 per share. State law requires that large stock dividends be capitalized at par value per share.

GENERAL JOURNAL — Page 71

Date		Description	PR	Debit	Credit
Dec	31	Stock Dividend Declared		20,000	
		Common Stock Dividend Distributable			20,000

50,000 × 40% = 20,000 shares × $1 par value = $20,000

Subsequent entries for large stock dividends are similar to those for small stock dividends.

Stock Splits

A distribution of additional shares of stock to stockholders according to their percent ownership.

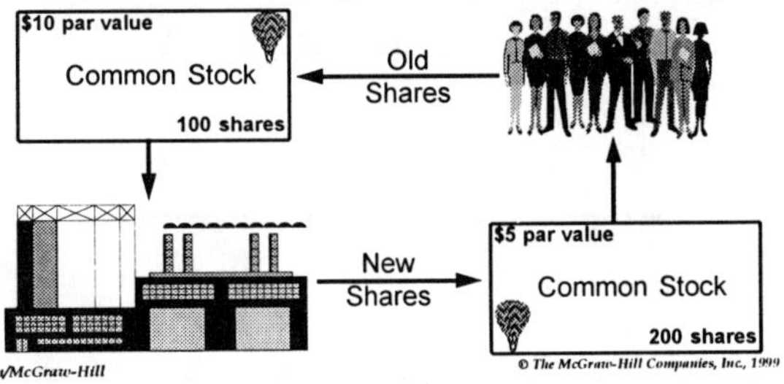

Stock Splits

TolTec, Inc. shows the following stockholders' equity section just prior to a 2-for-1 stock split.

TolTec, Inc. Stockholders' Equity June 30, 1999	
Common stock - $10 par value,	
100,000 shares authorized,	
25,000 shares issued and outstanding	$ 250,000
Contributed capital in excess of par value	300,000
Total contributed capital	550,000
Retained earnings	775,000
Total stockholders' equity	$ 1,325,000

Stock Splits

After the 2-for-1 split the stockholders' equity section of the balance sheet looks like this . . .

TolTec, Inc. Stockholders' Equity June 30, 1999	
Common stock - $10 par value,	
100,000 shares authorized,	
25,000 shares issued and outstanding	$ 250,000
Contributed capital in excess of par value	300,000
Total contributed capital	550,000
Retained earnings	775,000
Total stockholders' equity	$ 1,325,000

No accounting entry is made.

Treasury Stock

Corporations Acquiring Shares of Their Own Stock

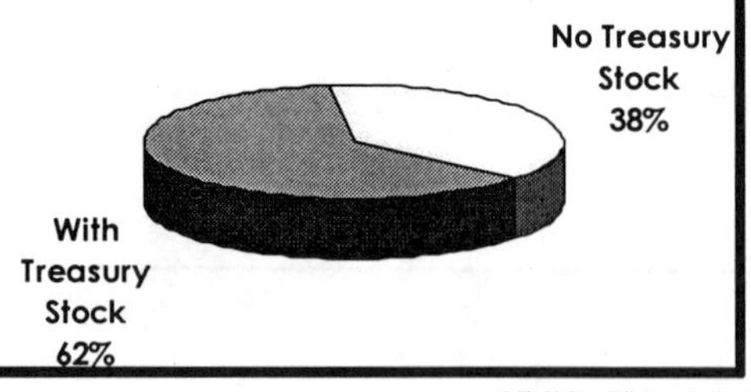

Treasury Stock

Corporations acquire shares of their own stock.

Why would a company do that?

✓Use the shares to acquire control of another corporation.

✓To avoid a hostile takeover.

✓Use the shares for employee stock options.

Purchasing Treasury Stock

On May, 8, 1999, Whitt, Inc. purchased 2,000 of its own shares of stock in the open market for $8,000. Let's prepare the entry to record the purchase.

GENERAL JOURNAL Page 71

Date		Description	PR	Debit	Credit
May	8				

Purchasing Treasury Stock

On May, 8, 1999, Whitt, Inc. purchased 2,000 of its own shares of stock in the open market for $8,000. Let's prepare the entry to record the purchase.

GENERAL JOURNAL Page 71

Date		Description	PR	Debit	Credit
May	8	Treasury Stock, Common		8,000	
		Cash			8,000

Treasury stock is shown as a reduction in total stockholders' equity on the balance sheet.

Selling Treasury Stock at Cost

On June 30, 1999, Whitt, Inc. sold 100 shares of its previously acquired treasury stock for $4 per share ($8,000 ÷ 2,000 shares). Let's prepare the entry.

GENERAL JOURNAL				Page 71	
Date		Description	PR	Debit	Credit
Jun	30				

Selling Treasury Stock at Cost

On June 30, 1999, Whitt, Inc. sold 100 shares of its previously acquired treasury stock for $4 per share ($8,000 ÷ 2,000 shares). Let's prepare the entry.

GENERAL JOURNAL				Page 71	
Date		Description	PR	Debit	Credit
Jun	30	Cash		400	
		Treasury Stock, Common			400

Selling Treasury Stock Above Cost

On July 19, 1999, Whitt, Inc. sold an additional 500 shares of its treasury stock for $8 per share.

GENERAL JOURNAL				Page 24	
Date		Description	PR	Debit	Credit
Jul	19	Cash		4,000	
		Treasury Stock, Common			2,000
		Contributed Capital, Treasury			
		Stock Transactions			2,000

	Shares	Per Share	Total
Sale	500	$ 8.00	$ 4,000
Cost	500	4.00	2,000
Contributed capital			$ 2,000

Selling Treasury Stock Below Cost

On August 27, 1999, Whitt sold an additional 400 shares of its treasury stock for $1.50 per share.

GENERAL JOURNAL					Page 44
Date		Description	PR	Debit	Credit
Aug	27				

Selling Treasury Stock Below Cost

On August 27, 1999, Whitt sold an additional 400 shares of its treasury stock for $1.50 per share.

GENERAL JOURNAL					Page 44
Date		Description	PR	Debit	Credit
Aug	27	Cash		600	
		Contributed Capital, Treasury			
		Stock Transactions		1,000	
		Treasury Stock			1,600

	Shares	Per Share	Total
Cost	400	$ 4.00	$ 1,600
Sale	400	1.50	600
Difference			$ 1,000

Reporting Income Information

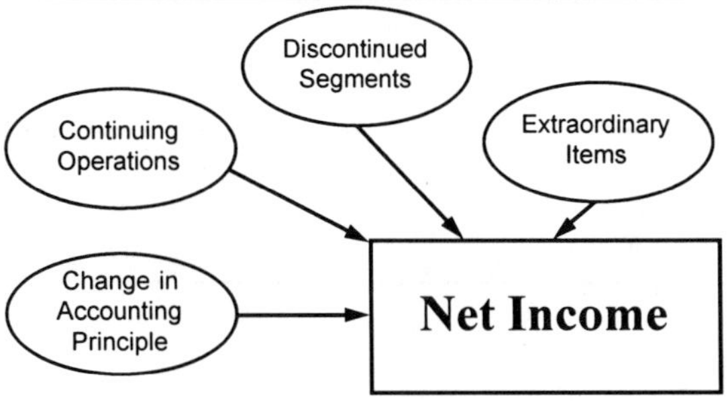

Reporting Income Information

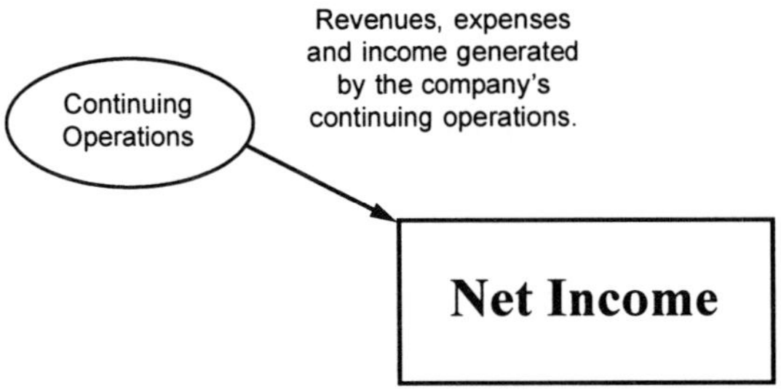

Reporting Income Information

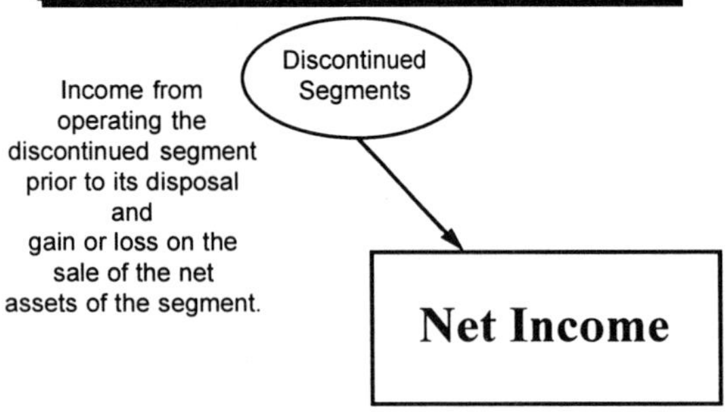

Reporting Income Information

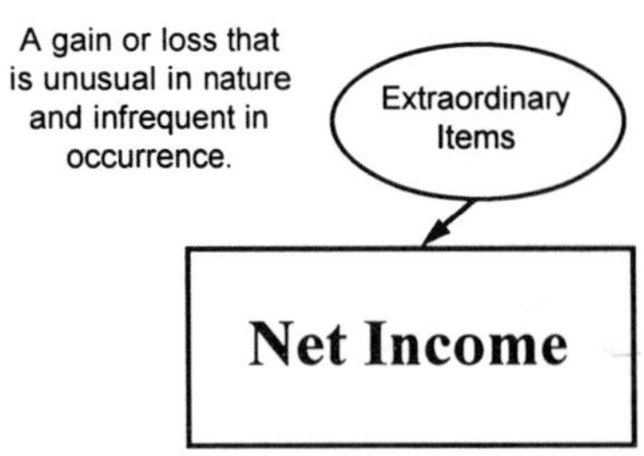

Reporting Income Information

The increase or decrease in income when changing from one generally accepted accounting principle to another.

Change in Accounting Principle → **Net Income**

Reporting Income Information

Campus, Inc.
Partial Income Statement
For Year Ended December 31, 1999

Income from continuing operations		$1,389,500
Discountinued operations:		
Income from operating Division A (net of $180,000 income taxes)	$420,000	
Loss on disposal of Division A (net of $66,000 tax benefit)	(154,000)	266,000
Extraordinary item:		
Loss from earthquake damage (net of $270,000 tax benefit)		(630,000)
Cumulative effect of a change in accounting principle:		
Effect on prior years' income of changing to a different depreciation method (net of $14,000 income taxes)		56,000
Net income		$1,081,500

Reporting on Changes in Accounting Principles

Campus, Inc. prepared the following schedule in connection with its change from double-declining balance to straight-line depreciation.

Prior to Change:	Double-Declining Depreciation	Straight-Line Depreciation	Pre-Tax Difference	After-Tax Cumulative Effect
1996	$ 90,000	$ 50,000		
1997	70,000	50,000		
1998	60,000	50,000		
	$ 220,000	$ 150,000	$ 70,000	$ 56,000
Year of Change:				
1999		35,000		
After Change:		35,000		

Campus is subject to a 20% income tax rate

Earnings Per Share

Earnings per share is one of the most widely cited items of accounting information.

$$\text{Basic earnings per share} = \frac{\text{Net income - Preferred dividends}}{\text{Weighted-average common shares outstanding}}$$

Changes in Common Shares Outstanding

Derby, Inc. reports net income of $75,000 and paid preferred dividends of $10,000 during 1999. The company started the year with 10,000 shares of common stock outstanding. Derby sold an additional 4,000 share of stock on March 31, and purchased 2,000 treasury shares on September 30, 1999. The weighted-average common shares outstanding is show below.

Date	Transaction	Outstanding Shares	Fraction of Year	Weighted Average
1/1/99	Balance	10,000	3/12	2,500
3/31/99	Sales of shares	14,000	6/12	7,000
9/30/99	Treasury shares	12,000	3/12	3,000
				12,500

Changes in Common Shares Outstanding

Derby, Inc. reports net income of $75,000 and paid preferred dividends of $10,000 during 1999. The company started the year with 10,000 shares of common stock outstanding. Derby sold an additional 4,000 share of stock on March 31, and purchased 2,000 treasury shares on September 30, 1999. The weighted-average common shares outstanding is show below.

$$\text{EPS} = \frac{\$75{,}000 - \$10{,}000}{12{,}500} = \$5.20$$

Complex Capital Structure

Capital structure includes dilutive securities such as:

- Stock options (rights to purchase common stock).
- Preferred stock convertible into common stock.

These items may reduce the basic earnings per share.

The company may be required to report basic and diluted earnings per share on the face of the income statement.

Stock Options

The right to purchase common stock at a fixed price over a specified period of time. As the stock's price rises above the fixed option price, the value of the option increases.

Option purchase price $30 per share.

Market price of stock $75 per share.

Stock Options

Options are given to key employees to motivate them to:

- focus on company performance,
- take a long-run perspective, and
- remain with the company.

Retained Earnings

Total cumulative amount of reported net income less any net losses and dividends declared since the company started operating.

Reed, Inc. Statement of Retained Earnings For Year Ended December 31, 1999	
Retained earnings, 1/1/99	$ 875,000
Plus: net income	155,600
Less: dividends declared	(80,000)
Retained earnings, 12/31/99	$ 950,600

Restricted Retained Earnings

Legal	Contractual
Most states restrict the amount of treasury stock purchases to the amount of retained earnings.	Loan agreement can include restrictions on paying dividends below a certain amount of retained earnings.

Appropriated Retained Earnings

A corporation's directors can voluntarily limit dividends because of a special need for cash such as the purchase of new facilities.

Reed, Inc. Statement of Retained Earnings For Year Ended December 31, 1999	
Retained earnings, 1/1/99	$ 875,000
Plus: net income	155,600
Less: dividends declared	(80,000)
Retained earnings, 12/31/99	$ 950,600
Appropriated retained earnings	(450,000)
Unappropriated retained earnings	$ 500,600

Prior Period Adjustments

Correction of material errors in past years' financial statements.

Reed, Inc.
Statement of Retained Earnings
For Year Ended December 31, 1999

Retained earnings, 1/1/99, as previously reported	$ 875,000
Prior period adjustment: Cost of equipment incorrectly expensed (net of $28,000 income taxes)	(72,000)
Retained earnings, 1/1/99, as adjusted	803,000
Plus: net income	155,600
Less: dividends declared	(80,000)
Retained earnings, 12/31/99	$ 878,600

Changes in Accounting Estimates

Many items reported in the financial statements are based on estimates. If new information comes to light that would cause us to change our estimate, we show the impact of the change in current and future periods.

Statement of Changes in Stockholders' Equity

Exh. 14-15

Intel
Statement of Changes in Stockholders' Equity
December 31, 1996

(In millions)	Common stock and capital in excess of par: Shares	Common stock and capital in excess of par: Amount	Retained Earnings	Total
Balance at December 30, 1995	821	$ 2,583	$ 9,557	$12,140
Stock sales	17	513		513
Stock repurchases and retirement	(17)	(269)	(925)	(1,194)
Cash dividends declared			(156)	(156)
Other, net		70	342	412
Net income			5,157	5,157
Balance at December 28, 1996	821	$ 2,897	$13,975	$16,872

Dividend Yield

Tells us the annual amount of cash dividends distributed to common stockholders relative to the stock's market price.

$$\textbf{Dividend Yield} = \frac{\textbf{Annual cash dividend per share}}{\textbf{Market value per share}}$$

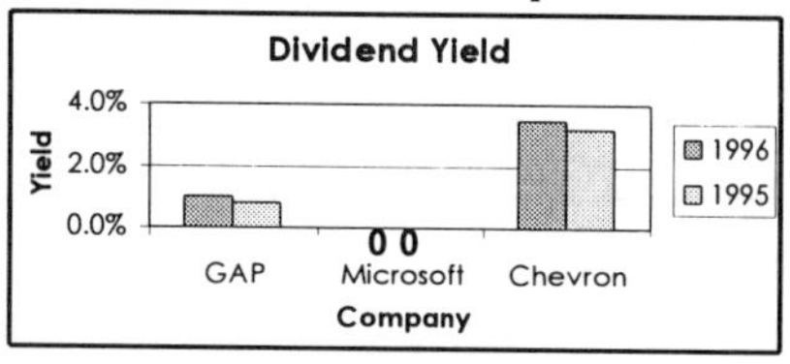

Price Earnings

This ratio reveals information about the stock market's expectations for a company's future growth in earnings, dividends, and opportunities.

$$\textbf{Price-Earnings} = \frac{\textbf{Market value per share}}{\textbf{Earnings per share}}$$

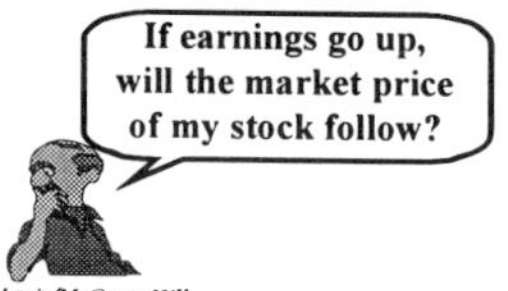

End of Chapter 14

15 CHAPTER Notes Payable and Bonds

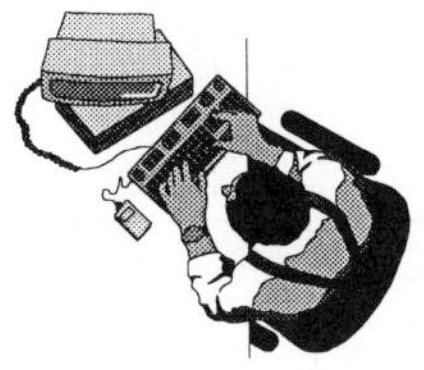

Basics of Bonds

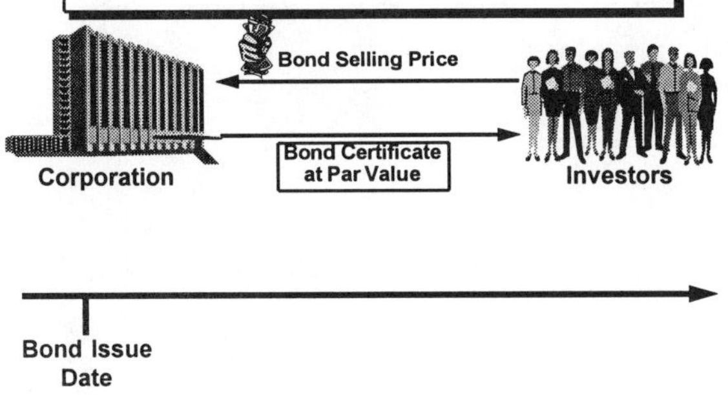

Basics of Bonds

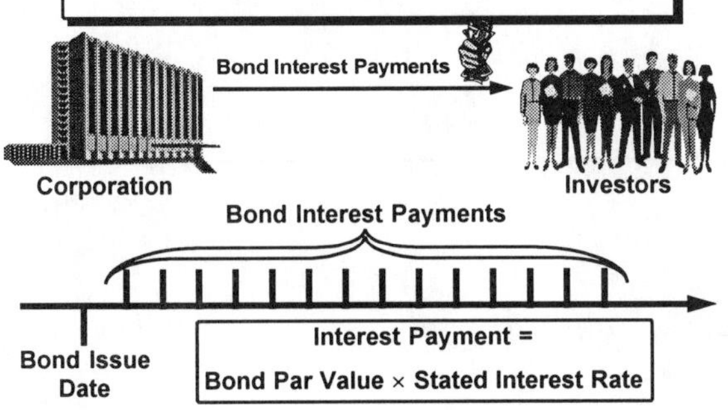

Basics of Bonds

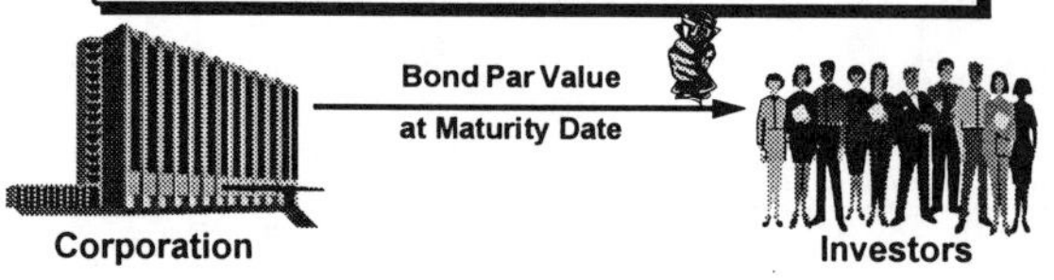

Advantages of Bonds

Bonds do not affect stockholder control.

Interest on bonds is tax deductible.

Bonds can increase return on equity.

Disadvantages of Bonds

Bonds require payment of both periodic interest and par value at maturity.

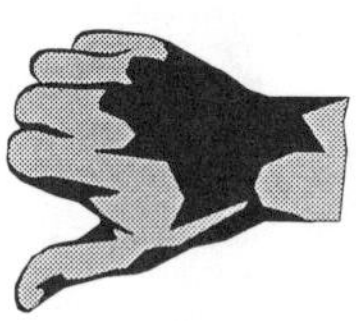

Bonds can decrease return on equity when the company pays more in interest than it earns on the borrowed funds.

Types of Bonds

- Secured and Unsecured
- Term and Serial
- Registered and Bearer
- Convertible and Callable

Bond Trading

Bond market values are expressed as a percent of their par value.

Bond Issuing Procedures

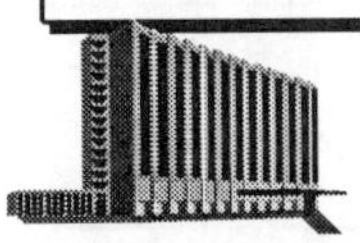

A company sells the bonds to. . .

. . .an investment firm called an underwriter. The underwriter sells the bonds to. . .

. . . investors

A trustee monitors the bond issue.

Issuing Bonds at Par

Prepare the entry for Jan. 1, 2000 to record the following bond issue by King Co.

Par Value = $1,000,000
Stated Interest Rate = 10%
Interest Dates = 6/30 & 12/31
Bond Date = Jan. 1, 2000
Maturity Date = Dec. 31, 2019 (20 years)

Issuing Bonds at Par

GENERAL JOURNAL — **Page 34**

Date		Description	PR	Debit	Credit
Jan.	1	Cash		1,000,000	
		Bonds Payable			1,000,000

Prepare the entry to record the semi-annual interest payment for June 30, 2000.

Issuing Bonds at Par

GENERAL JOURNAL — **Page 39**

Date		Description	PR	Debit	Credit
Jun.	30	Bond Interest Expense		50,000	
		Cash			50,000
		$1,000,000 × 10% × 1/2			

This entry will be made every six months until the bonds mature to record King Co.'s interest obligation.

Issuing Bonds at Par

On Dec. 31, 2019 when the bonds mature, King Co. would make the following entry.

GENERAL JOURNAL					Page 88
Date		Description	PR	Debit	Credit
Dec.	31	Bonds Payable		1,000,000	
		Cash			1,000,000

Exh. 15.3

Determining Bond Discount or Premium

Contract rate is:	Bond sells:
Above market rate	At a premium
Equal to market rate	At par value
Below market rate	At a discount

Next, let's look at issuing a bond at a discount.

Issuing Bonds at a Discount

Prepare the entry for Jan. 1, 2000 to record the following bond issue by Rose Co.

Par Value = $1,000,000
Issue Price = 92.6405% of par value
Stated Interest Rate = 10%
Market Interest Rate = 12%
Interest Dates = 6/30 & 12/31
Bond Date = Jan. 1, 2000
Maturity Date = Dec. 31, 2004 (5 years)

Issuing Bonds at a Discount

Par Value		Cash Proceeds		Discount
$1,000,000	-	$926,405	=	$ 73,595

$1,000,000 × 92.6405%

Amortizing the discount increases Interest Expense over the outstanding life of the bond.

Issuing Bonds at a Discount

On Jan. 1, 2000 Rose Co. would record the bond issue as follows.

GENERAL JOURNAL — Page 3

Date		Description	PR	Debit	Credit
Jan.	1	Cash		926,405	
		Discount on Bonds Payable		73,595	
		Bonds Payable			1,000,000

Contra-Liability Account

Issuing Bonds at a Discount

Partial Balance Sheet as of Jan. 1, 2000

Long-term Liabilities:		
Bonds Payable	$1,000,000	
Less: Discount on Bonds Payable	73,595	$926,405

Maturity Value

Carrying Value

Issuing Bonds at a Discount

Partial Balance Sheet as of Jan. 1, 2000

Long-term Liabilities:		
Bonds Payable	$ 1,000,000	
Less: Discount on Bonds Payable	73,595	$ 926,405

Using the straight-line method, the discount amortization will be $7,360 every six months.

$73,595 ÷ 10 periods = $7,360 (rounded)

Prepare the entry to record the semi-annual interest payment for June 30, 2000.

Issuing Bonds at a Discount

This entry will be made every six months to record the interest payment and the amortization of the discount.

GENERAL JOURNAL Page 33

Date		Description	PR	Debit	Credit
Jun.	30	Interest Expense		57,360	
		Discount on Bonds Payable			7,360
		Cash			50,000

$73,595 ÷ 10 periods = $7,360 (rounded)

$1,000,000 × 10% × ½ = $50,000

Straight-Line Amortization Table

Date	A Interest Payment	B Interest Expense	C Discount Amortization*	D Unamortized Discount	E Carrying Value
1/1/00				$ 73,595	$ 926,405
6/30/00	$ 50,000	$ 57,360	$ 7,360	66,235	933,765
12/31/01	50,000	57,360	7,360	58,875	941,125

A = $1,000,000 × 10% × ½ = $50,000
B = $50,000 + $7,360 = $57,360
C = $73,595 ÷ 10 = $7,395.50 rounded to $7,360
D = $66,235 - $7,360 = $58,875
E = $1,000,000 - $58,875 = $941,125

* Rounded.

Straight-Line Amortization Table

Date	A Interest Payment	B Interest Expense	C Discount Amortization*	D Unamortized Discount	E Carrying Value
1/1/00				$ 73,595	$ 926,405
6/30/00	$ 50,000	$ 57,360	$ 7,360	66,235	933,765
12/31/01	50,000	57,360	7,360	58,875	941,125
6/30/01	50,000	57,360	7,360	51,515	948,485
12/31/01	50,000	57,360	7,360	44,155	955,845
6/30/02	50,000	57,360	7,360	36,795	963,205
12/31/02	50,000	57,360	7,360	29,435	970,565
6/30/03	50,000	57,360	7,360	22,075	977,925
12/31/03	50,000	57,360	7,360	14,715	985,285
6/30/04	50,000	57,360	7,360	7,355	992,645
12/31/04	50,000	57,355	7,355	0	1,000,000
	$ 500,000	$ 573,595	$ 73,595		

* Rounded.

Straight-Line Method

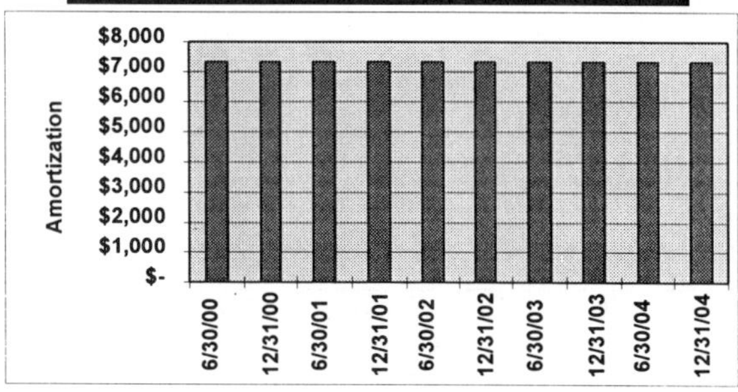

Effective Interest Method

The effective interest method allocates bond interest expense over the life of the bonds in a way that yields a constant rate of interest.

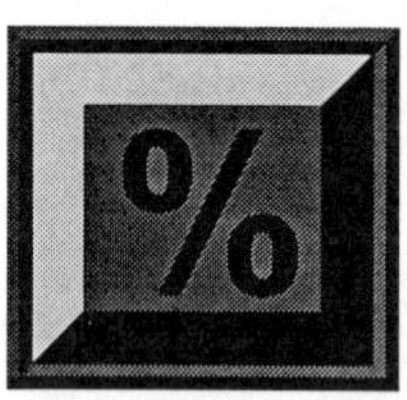

Effective Interest Amortization Table

Date	A Interest Payment	B Interest Expense*	C Discount Amortization*	D Unamortized Discount	E Present Value
1/1/00				$ 73,595	$ 926,405
6/30/00	$ 50,000	$ 55,584	$ 5,584	68,011	931,989
12/31/00	50,000	55,919	5,919	62,092	937,908

A: $1,000,000 × 10% × ½ = $50,000
B: $931,989 × 12% × ½ = $55,919
C: $55,919 - $50,000 = $5,919
D: $68,011 - $5,919 = $62,092
E: $1,000,000 - $62,092 = $937,908

* Rounded.

Effective Interest Amortization Table

Date	A Interest Payment	B Interest Expense*	C Discount Amortization*	D Unamortized Discount	E Present Value
1/1/00				$ 73,595	$ 926,405
6/30/00	$ 50,000	$ 55,584	$ 5,584	68,011	931,989
12/31/00	50,000	55,919	5,919	62,092	937,908
6/30/01	50,000	56,274	6,274	55,818	944,182
12/31/01	50,000	56,650	6,650	49,168	950,832
6/30/02	50,000	57,049	7,049	42,119	957,881
12/31/02	50,000	57,472	7,472	34,647	965,353
6/30/03	50,000	57,921	7,921	26,726	973,274
12/31/03	50,000	58,396	8,396	18,330	981,670
6/30/04	50,000	58,900	8,900	9,430	990,570
12/31/04	50,000	59,430	9,430	0	1,000,000
	$ 500,000	$ 573,595	$ 73,595		

* Rounded.

Effective Interest Method

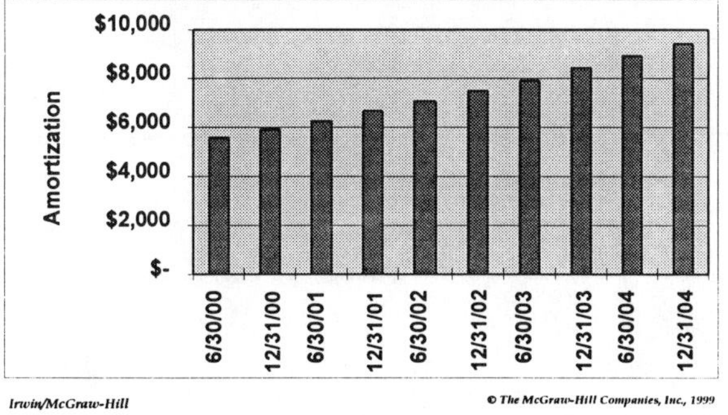

Comparing the Straight-Line and Effective Interest Methods

Both methods report the same amount of interest expense over the life of the bond.

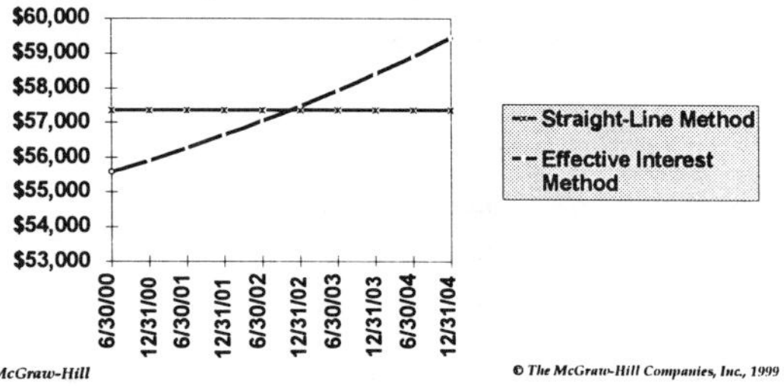

Issuing Bonds at a Premium

Prepare the entry for Jan. 1, 2000 to record the following bond issue by Rose Co.

Par Value = $1,000,000
Issue Price = 108.1145% of par value
Stated Interest Rate = 10%
Market Interest Rate = 8%
Interest Dates = 6/30 & 12/31
Bond Date = Jan. 1, 2000
Maturity Date = Dec. 31, 2004 (5 years)

Issuing Bonds at a Premium

Cash Proceeds		Par Value		Premium
$1,081,145	-	$ 1,000,000	=	$ 81,145

$1,000,000 × 108.1145%

Amortizing the premium decreases Interest Expense over the outstanding life of the bond.

Issuing Bonds at a Premium

On Jan. 1, 2000 Rose Co. would record the bond issue as follows.

GENERAL JOURNAL Page 3

Date		Description	PR	Debit	Credit
Jan.	1	Cash		1,081,145	
		Premium on Bonds Payable			81,145
		Bonds Payable			1,000,000

Adjunct-Liability Account

Issuing Bonds at a Premium

Partial Balance Sheet as of Jan. 1, 2000

Long-term Liabilities:		
Bonds Payable	$1,000,000	
Add: Premium on Bonds Payable	81,145	$ 1,081,145

Using the straight-line method, the premium amortization will be $8,115 every six months.

$81,145 ÷ 10 periods = $8,115 (rounded)

Prepare the entry to record the semi-annual interest payment for June 30, 2000.

Issuing Bonds at a Premium

This entry will be made every six months to record the interest payment and the amortization of the discount.

GENERAL JOURNAL Page 33

Date		Description	PR	Debit	Credit
Jun.	30	Interest Expense		41,885	
		Premium on Bonds Payable		8,115	
		Cash			50,000

$81,145 ÷ 10 periods = $8,115 (rounded)

$1,000,000 × 10% × ½ = $50,000

Straight-Line Amortization Table					
	A	B	C	D	E
Date	Interest Payment	Interest Expense	Premium Amortization*	Unamortized Premium	Carrying Value
1/1/00				$ 81,145	$ 1,081,145
6/30/00	$ 50,000	$ 41,885	$ 8,115	73,030	1,073,030
12/31/01	50,000	41,885	8,115	64,915	1,064,915
6/30/01	50,000	41,885	8,115	56,800	1,056,800
12/31/01	50,000	41,885	8,115	48,685	1,048,685
6/30/02	50,000	41,885	8,115	40,570	1,040,570
12/31/02	50,000	41,885	8,115	32,455	1,032,455
6/30/03	50,000	41,885	8,115	24,340	1,024,340
12/31/03	50,000	41,885	8,115	16,225	1,016,225
6/30/04	50,000	41,885	8,115	8,110	1,008,110
12/31/04	50,000	41,890	8,110	0	1,000,000
	$500,000	$418,855	$ 81,145		

* Rounded.

Effective Interest Method Amortization Table					
	A	B	C	D	E
Date	Interest Payment	Interest Expense*	Premium Amortization*	Unamortized Premium	Present Value
1/1/00				$ 81,145	$ 1,081,145
6/30/00	$ 50,000	$ 43,246	$ 6,754	74,391	1,074,391
12/31/00	50,000	42,976	7,024	67,367	1,067,367
6/30/01	50,000	42,695	7,305	60,062	1,060,062
12/31/01	50,000	42,402	7,598	52,464	1,052,464
6/30/02	50,000	42,099	7,901	44,563	1,044,563
12/31/02	50,000	41,783	8,217	36,346	1,036,346
6/30/03	50,000	41,454	8,546	27,800	1,027,800
12/31/03	50,000	41,112	8,888	18,912	1,018,912
6/30/04	50,000	40,756	9,244	9,668	1,009,668
12/31/04	50,000	40,332	9,668	0	1,000,000
	$ 500,000	$ 418,855	$ 81,145		

* Rounded.

Issuing Bonds Between Interest Dates

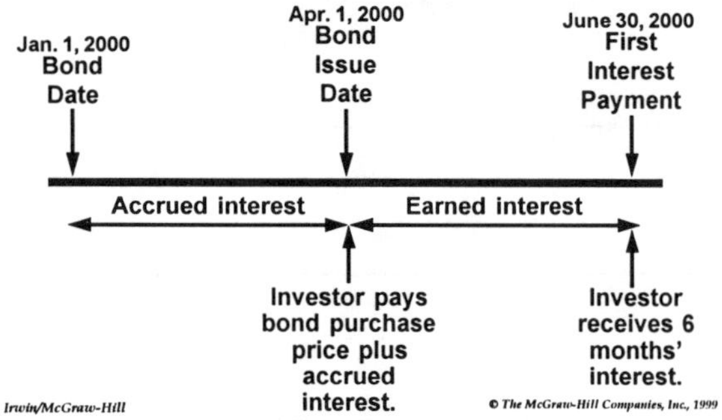

Issuing Bonds Between Interest Dates

Prepare the entry to record the following bond issue by FishCo on Apr. 1, 2000.

Par Value = $1,000,000
Stated Interest Rate = 10%
Market Interest Rate = 10%
Interest Dates = 6/30 & 12/31
Bond Date = Jan. 1, 2000
Maturity Date = Dec. 31, 2004 (5 years)

Issuing Bonds Between Interest Dates

How much cash is FishCo going to receive for the entire issue of the bonds?

Issue Price of Bonds	$ 1,000,000
Accrued Interest $1,000,000 × 10% × $^3/_{12}$ =	25,000
Total Cash Received	$ 1,025,000

Issuing Bonds Between Interest Dates

What does the $25,000 in accrued interest represent for FishCo?

Prepare the journal entry to record FishCo's bond issue on April 1, 2000.

Issuing Bonds Between Interest Dates

Here is the journal entry to record FishCo's bond issue on April 1, 2000.

GENERAL JOURNAL					Page 33
Date		Description	PR	Debit	Credit
Apr.	1	Cash		1,025,000	
		Interest Payable			25,000
		Bonds Payable			1,000,000

Now, prepare the entry for June 30, 2000.

Issuing Bonds Between Interest Dates

Here is the entry to record FishCo's interest payment on June 30, 2000.

GENERAL JOURNAL					Page 43
Date		Description	PR	Debit	Credit
Jun.	30	Interest Payable		25,000	
		Interest Expense		25,000	
		Cash			50,000

$1,000,000 × 10% × ½ = $50,000

Accruing Bond Interest Expense

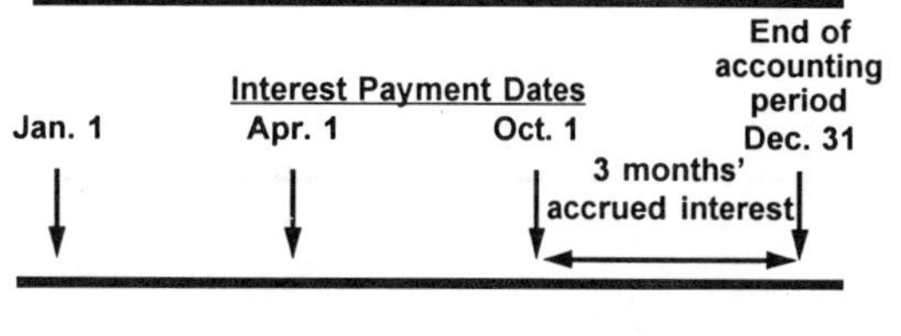

At year-end, an adjusting entry is necessary to recognize bond interest expense accrued since the most recent interest payment.

Present Value of a Discount Bond

Calculate the issue price of Roses Inc.'s bonds.

Par Value = $1,000,000
Issue Price = ?
Stated Interest Rate = 10%
Market Interest Rate = 12%
Interest Dates = 6/30 & 12/31
Bond Date = Jan. 1, 2000
Maturity Date = Dec. 31, 2004 (5 years)

Present Value of a Discount Bond

Cash Flow	Table	Table Value	Amount	Present Value
Par value of the bond	PV of $1			
Interest (annuity)	PV of an Annuity of $1			
Price of bond				

1. Semiannual rate = 6% (Market rate 12% ÷ 2)
2. Semiannual periods = 10 (Bond life 5 years × 2)

Bond Retirement

➢ **At Maturity**

GENERAL JOURNAL — Page 43

Date		Description	PR	Debit	Credit
Dec.	31	Bonds Payable		1,000,000	
		Cash			1,000,000

➢ **Before Maturity**

- **Carrying Value > Retirement Price = Gain**
- **Carrying Value < Retirement Price = Loss**

Long-Term Notes Payable

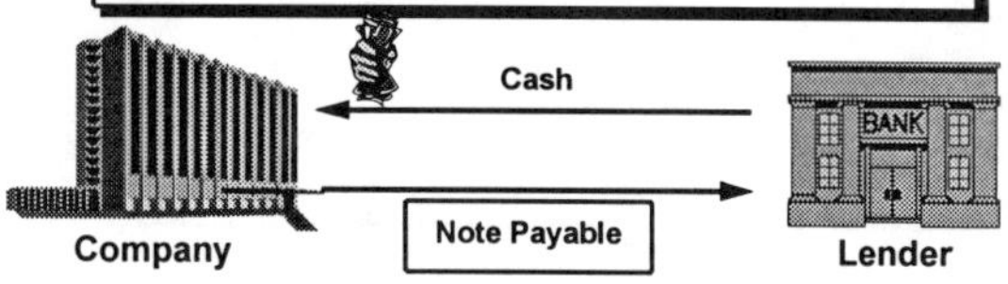

When is the repayment of the principal and interest going to be made?

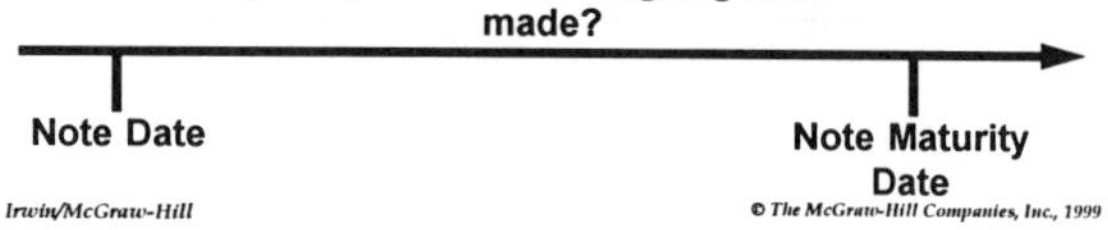

Long-Term Notes Payable

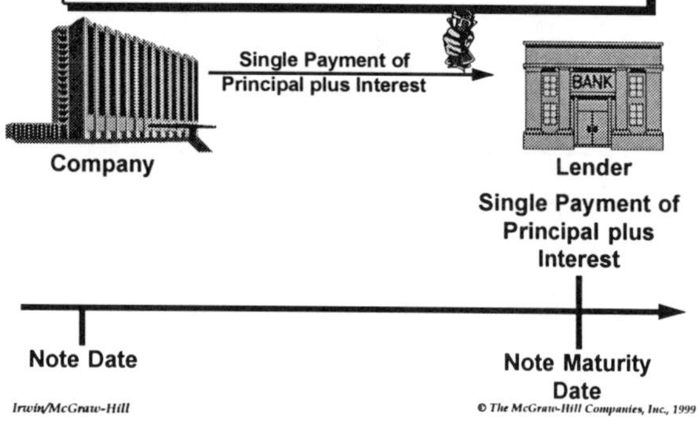

Interest-Bearing Note with Interest Paid at Maturity

Local Co. borrows $25,000 at 10% with payment of the principal and interest at the end of three years.

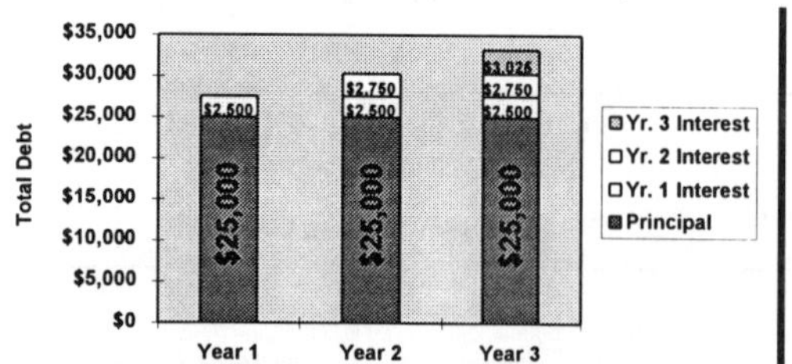

Payment at end of year 3 is $33,275.

Installment Notes Payable

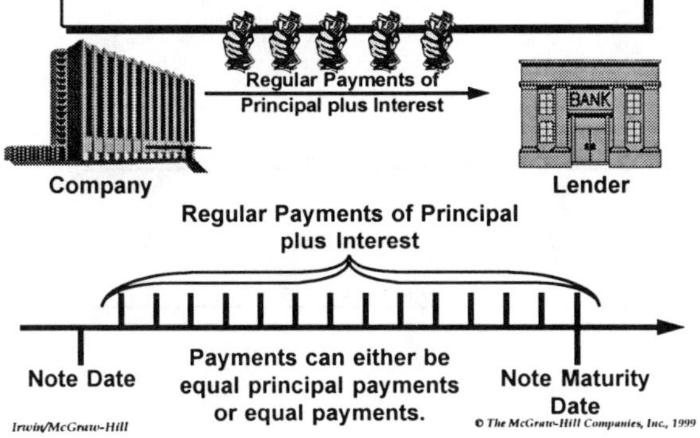

Installment Notes Payable
Equal Principal Payments

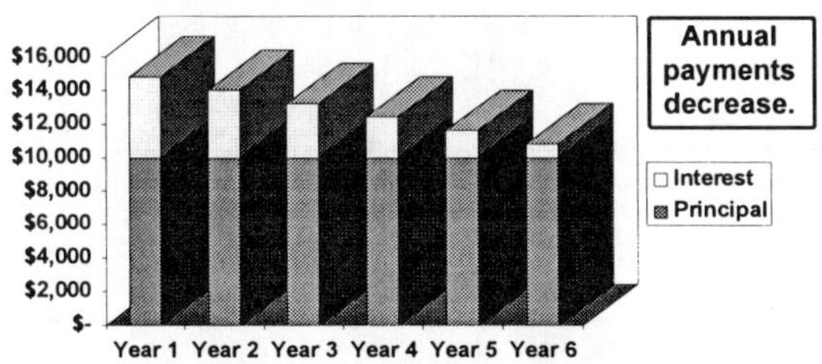

The principal payments are $10,000 each year.
Interest expense decreases each year.

Installment Notes Payable
Equal Payments

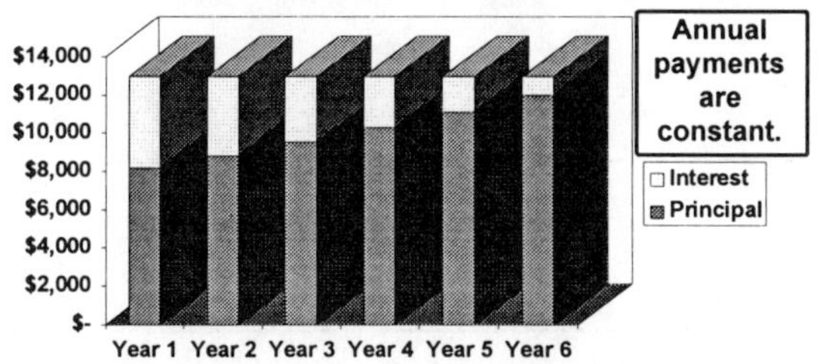

The principal payments increase each year.
Interest expense decreases each year.

Mortgage Notes

- **A legal agreement that helps protect the lender if the borrower fails to make the required payments.**
- **Gives the lender the right to be paid out of the cash proceeds from the sale of the borrower's assets specifically identified in the mortgage contract.**

Exh. 15.21

Pledged Assets to Secured Liabilities

$$\text{Pledged Assets to Secured Liabilities} = \frac{\text{Book Value of Pledged Assets}}{\text{Book Value of Secured Liabilities}}$$

This ratio helps creditors determine whether the pledged assets of a debtor provide adequate security for secured debt obligations.

16 CHAPTER

Long-Term Investments and International Accounting

Classifying Investments

Short-Term versus Long-Term

Short-Term Investments

Usually held as an investment of cash for use in current operations.

A current asset that is readily convertible into cash.

Irwin/McGraw-Hill
© The McGraw-Hill Companies, Inc., 1999

Classifying Investments

Short-Term versus Long-Term

Long-Term Investments

Bonds or stock that are not marketable or, if marketable, aren't intended to be converted into cash in the short-term.

Irwin/McGraw-Hill
© The McGraw-Hill Companies, Inc., 1999

Proper Accounting for Long-Term Investments

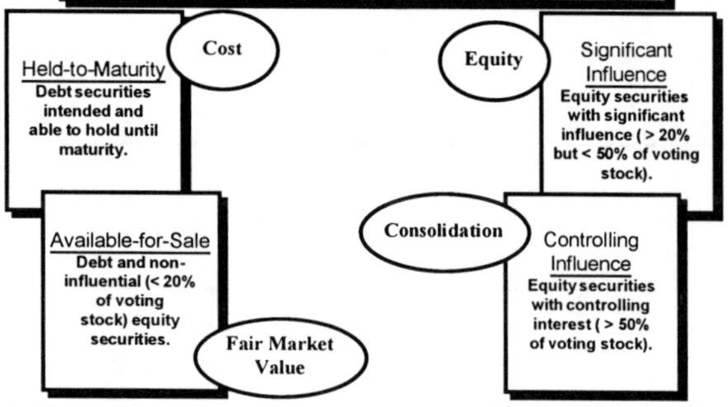

Held-to-maturity Securities

On January 1, 1998, Eagle, Co. purchased $50,000 par value of Potter Co. bonds for $50,000 cash. The bonds pay interest semiannually on June 30 and December 31 at the rate of 9%. Let's record Eagle's purchase of the bonds.

GENERAL JOURNAL — Page 34

Date		Description	PR	Debit	Credit
Jan	1				

Held-to-maturity Securities

On June 30, 1998, Eagle receives its first interest check from Potter.

GENERAL JOURNAL — Page 67

Date		Description	PR	Debit	Credit
Jun	30				

Available-for-sale Securities

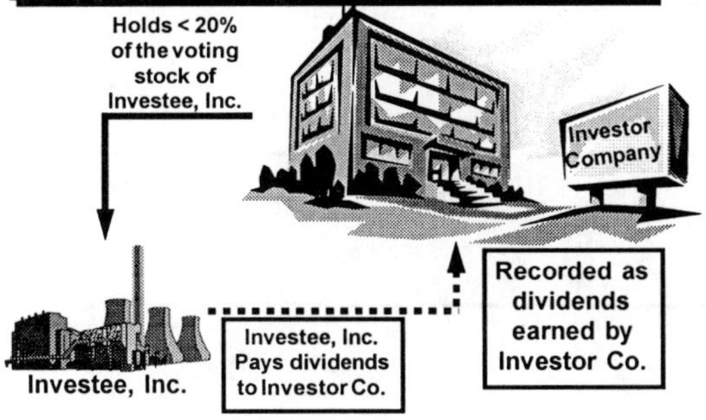

Available-for-sale Securities

WestCo purchases 10% of the voting common stock of Warren, Inc. for $1,000,000 cash. WestCo treats the securities as available for sale. What is the balance in WestCo's Investment account?

a. $1,200,000
b. $1,020,000
c. $1,000,000
d. $ 970,000

Available-for-sale Securities

Warren declares and pays total dividends of $100,000 and reports income of $300,000. How much income will WestCo recognize?

a. $300,000
b. $100,000
c. $30,000
d. $10,000

Available-for-sale Securities

Let's prepare the entry to record the receipt of the dividend from Warren, Inc.

GENERAL JOURNAL Page 2

Date		Description	PR	Debit	Credit

Available-for-sale Securities

WestCo sold one-half of its investment in Warren, Inc. for $575,000 cash. Let's record this transaction.

GENERAL JOURNAL Page 2

Date		Description	PR	Debit	Credit

Reporting Fair Market Value of Available-for-sale Securities

On the balance sheet date, the fair market value of the Warren stock owned by WestCo was $590,000. WestCo adjusts its investment to reflect this unrealized holding gain.

GENERAL JOURNAL Page 2

Date		Description	PR	Debit	Credit

Reporting Fair Market Value of Available-for-sale Securities

WestCo's balance sheet would contain the following:

Assets:	
Long-term investments:	
Available-for-sale securities (at fair market value)	**$ 590,000**
Stockholders' equity	
Unrealized holding gain	**$ 90,000**

Investment in Equity Securities with Significant Influence

Investment in Equity Securities with Significant Influence

Investment in Equity Securities

WestCo purchases 25% of Adams, Inc. for $1,000,000 cash and has significant influence. What is the balance in WestCo's investment account?

a. $1,200,000
b. $1,050,000
c. $1,000,000
d. $ 800,000

Investment in Equity Securities

Adams reports income of $500,000. What is the balance in WestCo's investment account?

a. $1,500,000
b. $1,125,000
c. $1,000,000
d. $ 875,000

Investment in Equity Securities

Let's make the entry to recognize the increase in the investment account.

GENERAL JOURNAL Page 17

Date		Description	PR	Debit	Credit

Investment in Equity Securities

Let's make the entry to recognize the increase in the investment account.

GENERAL JOURNAL					Page 17
Date		Description	PR	Debit	Credit
		Investment in Adams Stock		125,000	
		Earnings from Investment			125,000
		To record share of Adams income.			

Investment in Equity Securities

Now, Adams pays total dividends of $100,000. What is the balance in WestCo's Investment account?

a. $ 900,000

b. $ 975,000

c. $1,000,000

d. $1,100,000

Equity Method

Now, let's record the receipt of dividends from Adams.

GENERAL JOURNAL					Page 17
Date		Description	PR	Debit	Credit

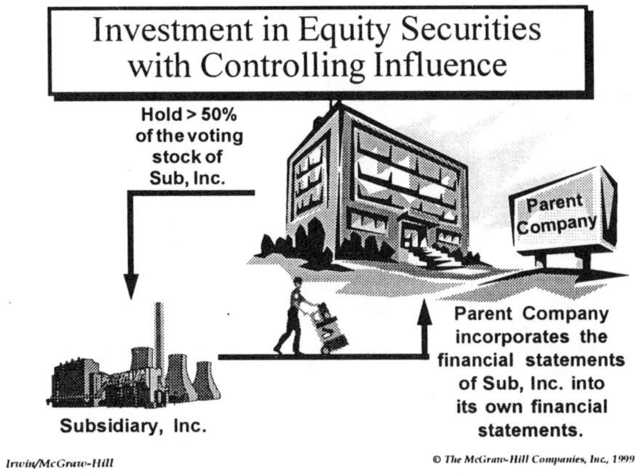
Investment in Equity Securities with Controlling Influence
Hold > 50% of the voting stock of Sub, Inc.
Parent Company
Parent Company incorporates the financial statements of Sub, Inc. into its own financial statements.
Subsidiary, Inc.
Irwin/McGraw-Hill
© The McGraw-Hill Companies, Inc, 1999

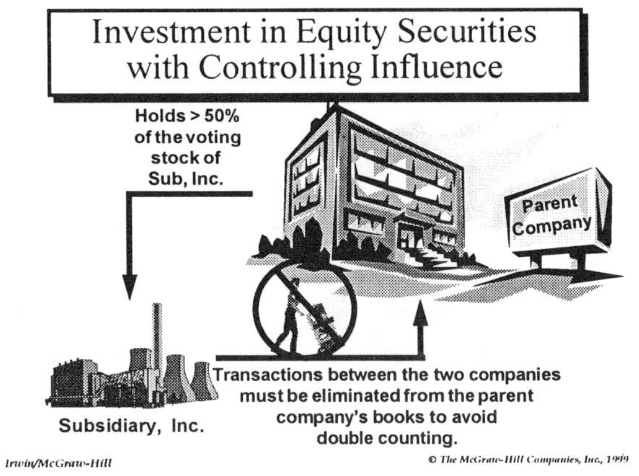
Investment in Equity Securities with Controlling Influence
Holds > 50% of the voting stock of Sub, Inc.
Parent Company
Transactions between the two companies must be eliminated from the parent company's books to avoid double counting.
Subsidiary, Inc.
Irwin/McGraw-Hill
© The McGraw-Hill Companies, Inc, 1999

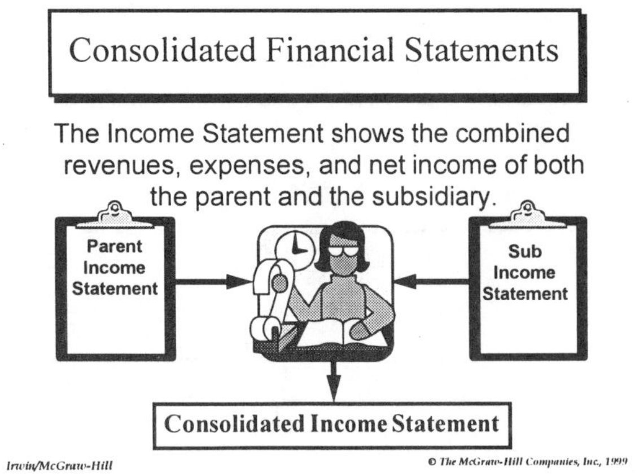
Consolidated Financial Statements
The Income Statement shows the combined revenues, expenses, and net income of both the parent and the subsidiary.
Parent Income Statement
Sub Income Statement
Consolidated Income Statement
Irwin/McGraw-Hill
© The McGraw-Hill Companies, Inc, 1999

Accounting for Investments in Securities

Exh. 16-7

Class of investment security	Accounting Method
Short-term:	
Held-to-maturity debt	Cost
Trading debt and equity	FMV
Available-for-sale debt and equity	FMV
Long-term:	
Held-to-maturity debt	Cost
Available-for-sale debt and equity	FMV
Equity without significant influence	Equity
Equity with controlling influence	Equity

Investments in International Operations

Let's look at some of the accounting problems we encounter when dealing with foreign currency.

Investments in International Operations

Two major challenges arise when companies have international operations.

1. Accounting for sales or purchases listed in a foreign currency.
2. Preparing consolidated financial statements with international subsidiaries.

Exh. 16-8

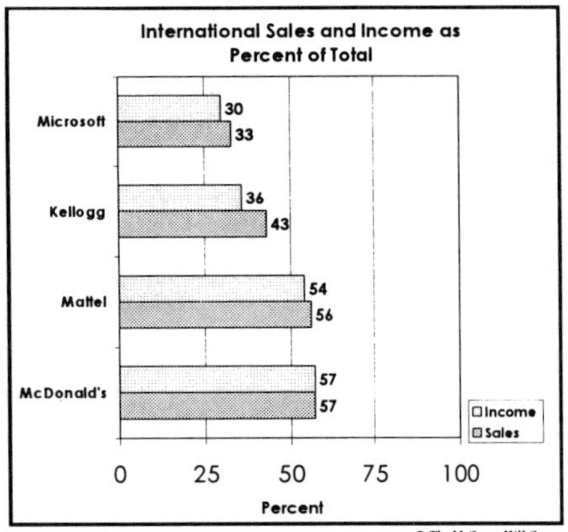

Exh. 16-9

Exchange Rates Between Currencies

We will use these exchange rates to illustrate accounting for sales and purchases.

Foreign Exchange Rates for Selected Currencies January 1, 1998			
Country (unit)	Price in $U.S.	Country (unit)	Price in $U.S.
Britain (pound)	$ 1.6508	Canada (dollar)	$ 0.6992
Germany (mark)	0.5562	France (franc)	0.1663
Mexico (peso)	0.1239	Japan (yen)	0.0077
Taiwan (dollar)	0.0306	Europe (ECU)	1.0991

Sales or Purchases Listed in a Foreign Currency

On January 1, 1998, Texas, Inc., a U.S. based manufacturer, made a credit sale to Royal, Ltd. a British retail company. The sale is listed as £30,000 and is due on January 19, 1999.

GENERAL JOURNAL Page 17

Date		Description	PR	Debit	Credit
Jan	1				

Sales or Purchases Listed in a Foreign Currency

On January 19, 1998, Texas, Inc., received a check from Royal, Ltd. for £30,000. The exchange rate at the end of the day is $1.7000 per pound.

GENERAL JOURNAL — Page 31

Date		Description	PR	Debit	Credit
Jan	19				

Consolidated Statements with International Subsidiaries

Before preparing consolidated statements, the parent must translate financial statements of its international subsidiary into U.S. dollars.

Income Statement Japanese, Inc. For Year Ended 12/31/99	
Sales	¥10,000,000

¥10,000,000
× .0077
$77,000

Income Statement U.S Company For Year Ended 12/31/99	
Income from Japanese, Inc.	$77,000

Return on Total Assets

Return on Total Assets = Profit Margin × Total Asset Turnover

$$\frac{\text{Net Income}}{\text{Average Total Assets}} = \frac{\text{Net Income}}{\text{Net Sales}} \times \frac{\text{Net Sales}}{\text{Average Total Assets}}$$

Profit Margin: Reflects the percent of net income in each dollar of net sales.

Total Asset Turnover: Reflects a company's ability to produce net sales from total assets.

Return on Total Assets

Exh. 16-11

Return on Total Assets	=	Profit Margin	×	Total Asset Turnover
Net Income / Average Total Assets	=	Net Income / Net Sales	×	Net Sales / Average Total Assets

$$\frac{\text{Net Income}}{\text{Average Total Assets}} = \frac{\text{Net Income}}{\text{Net Sales}} \times \frac{\text{Net Sales}}{\text{Average Total Assets}}$$

Reebok

Year	Return on Total Assets	=	Profit Margin	×	Total Asset Turnover
1996	8.06%	=	3.99%	×	2.02%
1995	9.98%	=	4.73%	×	2.11%
1994	16.76%	=	7.76%	×	2.16%

Irwin/McGraw-Hill

End of Chapter 16

Irwin/McGraw-Hill

17 CHAPTER Reporting and Analyzing Cash Flows

Measuring Cash Flows

Cash

Cash Equivalents → **Cash** ← **Currency**

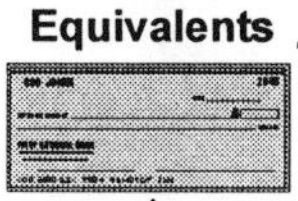

- Short-term, highly liquid investments.
- Readily convertible into cash.
- So near maturity that market value is unaffected by interest rate changes.

Classifying Cash Flows

The Statement of Cash Flows includes the following three sections:

- ➤ **Operating Activities**
- ➤ **Investing Activities**
- ➤ **Financing Activities**

❶ Operating Activities

Inflows include:
- Receipts from customers.
- Cash dividends received.
- Interest from borrowers.
- Other.

Outflows include:
- Salaries and wages.
- Payments to suppliers.
- Taxes and fines.
- Interest paid to lenders.
- Other.

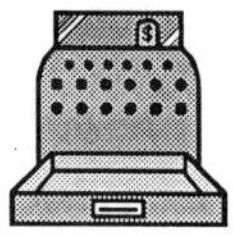

❷ Investing Activities

Inflows from:
- Selling long-term productive assets.
- Selling equity investments.
- Collecting of principal on loans.
- Other.

+

Outflows to:
- Purchase long-term productive assets.
- Purchase equity investments.
- Purchase debt investments.
- Make loans.

–

Cash Flows from Investing Activities

❸ Financing Activities

Inflows from:
- Issuing its own equity securities.
- Issuing bonds and notes.
- Issuing short-term and long-term liabilities.

+

Outflows to:
- Pay dividends to stockholders.
- Purchase treasury stock.
- Repay cash loans.
- Cover withdrawals by owners.

–

Cash Flows from Financing Activities

Noncash Investing and Financing Activities

Items requiring separate disclosure include:

- **Retirement of debt by issuing equity securities.**
- **Conversion of preferred stock to common stock.**
- **Leasing of assets in a capital lease transaction.**

Analyzing Noncash Accounts

The changes in cash can be determined by analyzing the noncash accounts on the balance sheet.

Δ Cash = Δ Liabilities + Δ Stockholders' Equity − Δ Noncash Assets

Derives from . . .

Assets = Liabilities + Stockholders' Equity

Direct Method Cash Received from Customers

Exh. 17.12

Can be computed two ways:

- Obtained from cash receipts journal.
- Obtained from accrual sales information.

Cash received from customers = Sales { - Increase in A/R; + Decrease in A/R }

Cash Received from Customers Question

The balance in A/R was $40,000 on 1/1/98 and the balance was $52,000 on 12/31/98. If total sales revenue for 1998 was $800,000, then how much cash was received from customers?

a. $800,000

b. $760,000

c. $812,000

d. $788,000

Direct Method Cash Paid for Merchandise

Exh. 17.13

- Step 1

Purchases = COGS { + Increase in inventory / - Decrease in inventory

- Step 2

Cash paid for merchandise = Purchases { + Decrease in A/P / - Increase in A/P

Cash Paid for Merchandise Question

How much did Lug Lite pay for inventory in 1997?

Inventory, 1/1/97	$130,000	A/P, 1/1/97	$ 23,000
Inventory, 12/31/97	$165,000	A/P, 12/31/97	$ 35,000
COGS, 12/31/97	$900,000		

a. $900,000
b. $923,000
c. $947,000
d. $877,000

Direct Method
Wages and Operating Expenses

Exh. 17.14

The cash paid for wages and other operating expenses is affected by

(1) whether the expense was prepaid, and

(2) whether the expense was accrued.

Cash paid for wages and other operating expenses = Wages and other operating expenses { + Increase in prepaid expenses / - Decrease in prepaid expenses } { + Decrease in accrued liabilities / - Increase in accrued liabilities }

Direct Method
Cash Paid for Interest and Taxes

Exh. 17.15

➢ Interest

Cash paid for interest = Interest Expense { + Decrease in interest payable / - Increase in interest payable }

➢ Taxes

Cash paid for taxes = Tax Expense { + Decrease in taxes payable / - Increase in taxes payable }

Direct Method
Depreciation Expense

➢ **Depreciation, Amortization, and Depletion Expenses**
- **Operating cash flows are not involved.**
- **They are not disclosed in the Statement of Cash Flows using the direct method.**

Direct Method
Gains and Losses

Gains and losses do not appear on the Statement of Cash Flows using the Direct Method.

Indirect Method of Reporting Operating Cash Flows

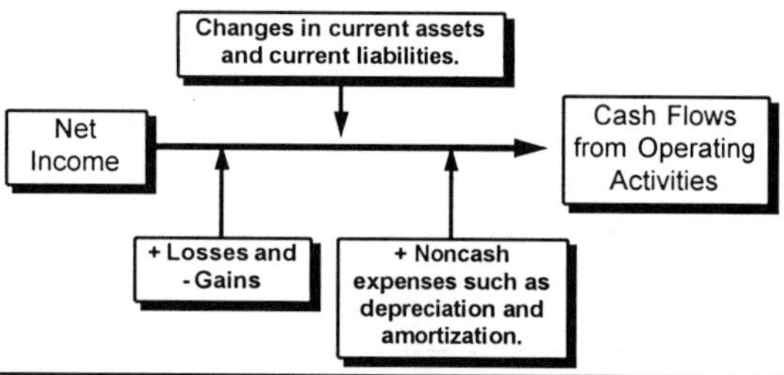

97.5% of all companies use the indirect method.

Indirect Method of Reporting Operating Cash Flows

	Change in Account Balance During Year	
	Increase	Decrease
Current Assets	Subtract from net income.	Add to net income.
Current Liabilities	Add to net income.	Subtract from net income.

Use this table when adjusting Net Income to Operating Cash Flows.

Indirect Method Example

East, Inc. reports $125,000 net income for the year ended December 31, 1999.

Accounts Receivable increased by $7,500 during the year and Accounts Payable increased by $10,000.

During 1999, East reported $12,500 of Depreciation Expense.

What is East, Inc.'s Operating Cash Flow for 1999?

Continue

Statement of Cash Flows Indirect Method Example

Joe's Place has prepared the Balance Sheet as of 3/31/98 and 3/31/97. The Income Statement for the year ended 3/31/98 has also been prepared. Joe needs help preparing the Statement of Cash Flows.

Statement of Cash Flows Indirect Method Example

Joe's Place
Income Statement
For the Year Ending 3/31/98

Revenues	$ 727,000
Operating Expenses	(748,000)
Depreciation Expense	(6,000)
Gain on Sale of Land	8,000
Net Loss	$ (19,000)

Statement of Cash Flows Indirect Method Example

The $8,000 gain was the result of selling land costing $32,000 for $40,000 during the period.

nt
/31/98

Revenues	$727,000
Operating Expenses	(748,000)
Depreciation Expense	(6,000)
Gain on Sale of Land	8,000
Net Loss	$ (19,000)

Statement of Cash Flows Indirect Method Example

Joe's Place
Balance Sheets

	3/31/97	3/31/98
Assets		
Cash	$ 90,000	$ 62,000
Accounts Receivable	40,000	23,000
Inventory	300,000	350,000
Land	112,000	80,000
Equipment, net	45,000	39,000
Total Assets	$ 587,000	$ 554,000

Statement of Cash Flows Indirect Method Example

Joe's Place
Balance Sheets (cont.)

	3/31/97	3/31/98
Liabilities		
Accounts Payable	$ 27,000	$ 38,000
Salaries Payable	14,000	9,000
Long-Term Note Payable	50,000	-
Total Liabilities	$ 91,000	$ 47,000
Owners' Equity		
Common Stock	$450,000	$500,000
Retained Earnings	46,000	7,000
Total Owners' Equity	$496,000	$507,000
Total Liabilities and OE	$587,000	$554,000

Statement of Cash Flows Indirect Method Example

Joe's Place issued $50,000 of nopar common stock to settle the $50,000 note payable.

	3/31/97	3/31/98
	27,000	$ 38,000
	14,000	9,000
Long-Term Note Payable	50,000	-
Total Liabilities	$ 91,000	$ 47,000
Owners' Equity		
Common Stock	$450,000	$500,000
Retained Earnings	46,000	7,000
Total Owners' Equity	$496,000	$507,000
Total Liabilities and OE	$587,000	$554,000

Statement of Cash Flows Indirect Method Example

Ending Retained Earnings at 3/31/98 was computed as follows:

	Beginning R/E, 3/31/97	$ 46,000
–	Net Loss for 1998	(19,000)
–	Dividends Paid in 1998	(20,000)
=	Ending R/E, 3/31/98	$ 7,000

		3/31/98
		$ 38,000
		9,000
		-
		$ 47,000
		$500,000
Retained Earnings	46,000	7,000
Total Owners' Equity	$496,000	$507,000
Total Liabilities and OE	$587,000	$554,000

Cash Flow on Total Assets

Exh. 17.20

Used, along with income-based ratios, to assess company performance.

$$\text{Cash Flow on Total Assets} = \frac{\text{Operating cash flows}}{\text{Average total assets}}$$

18 CHAPTER Analyzing Financial Statements

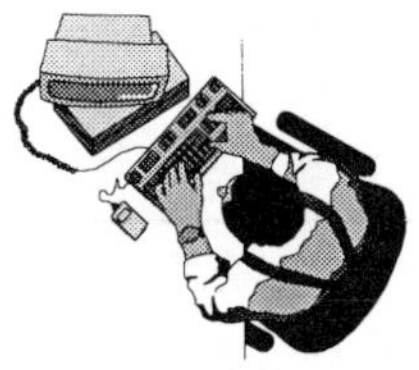

Basics of Analysis

Purpose of Analysis

Financial statement analysis helps users make better decisions.

Internal Users
Managers
Officers
Internal Auditors

External Users
Shareholders
Lenders
Customers

Building Blocks of Analysis

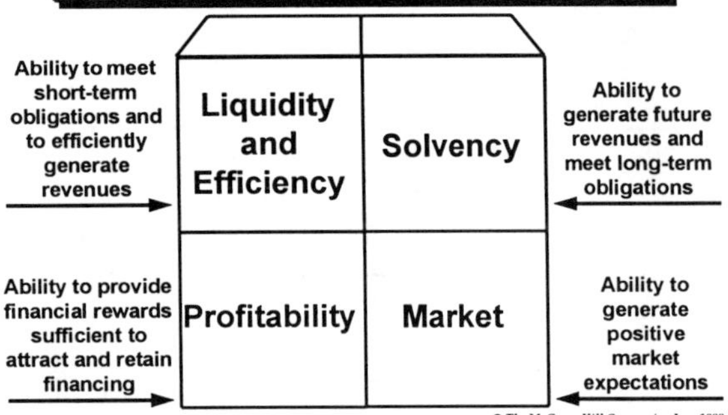

Information for Analysis

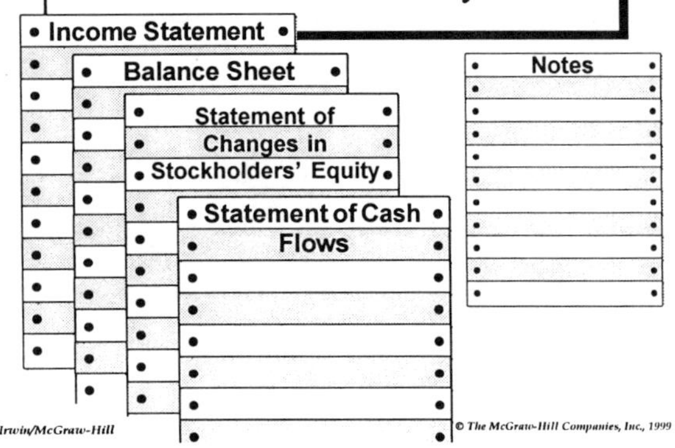

Standards for Comparison

❶ Intracompany

❷ Competitor

❸ Industry

❹ Guidelines

Tools of Analysis

Comparing a company's financial condition and performance across time

Tools of Analysis

Comparing a company's financial condition and performance to a base amount

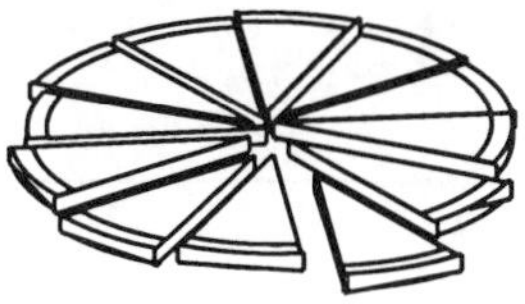

Tools of Analysis

Using key relations among financial statement items

Comparative Statements
Example

Let's look at Clover Corporation's comparative balance sheet and income statement for 1998 and 1997.

CLOVER CORPORATION
Comparative Balance Sheets
December 31,

	1998	1997	Dollar Change	Percent Change*
Assets				
Current assets:				
Cash and equivalents	$ 12,000	$ 23,500		
Accounts receivable, net	60,000	40,000		
Inventory	80,000	100,000		
Prepaid expenses	3,000	1,200		
Total current assets	$ 155,000	$ 164,700		
Property and equipment:				
Land	40,000	40,000		
Buildings and equipment, net	120,000	85,000		
Total property and equipment	$ 160,000	$ 125,000		
Total assets	$ 315,000	$ 289,700		

* Percent rounded to first decimal point.

Comparative Statements
Example

Calculate Change in Dollar Amount

Dollar Change = Analysis Period Amount − Base Period Amount

Since we are measuring the amount of the change between 1997 and 1998, the dollar amounts for 1997 become the "base" period amounts.

Comparative Statements
Example

Calculate Change as a Percent

$$\text{Percent Change} = \frac{\text{Dollar Change}}{\text{Base Period Amount}} \times 100\%$$

%

CLOVER CORPORATION
Comparative Balance Sheets
December 31,

	1998	1997	Dollar Change	Percent Change*
Assets				
Current assets:				
Cash and equivalents	$ 12,000	$ 23,500	$ (11,500)	(48.9)
Accounts receivable, net	60,000	40,000	20,000	50.0
Inventory	80,000	100,000	(20,000)	(20.0)
Prepaid expenses	3,000	1,200	1,800	150.0
Total current assets	$ 155,000	$ 164,700	$ (9,700)	(5.9)
Property and equipment:				
Land	40,000	40,000	-	0.0
Buildings and equipment, net	120,000	85,000	35,000	41.2
Total property and equipment	$ 160,000	$ 125,000	$ 35,000	28.0
Total assets	$ 315,000	$ 289,700	$ 25,300	8.7

* Percent rounded to first decimal point.

CLOVER CORPORATION
Comparative Balance Sheets
December 31,

	1998	1997	Dollar Change	Percent Change*
Liabilities and Shareholders' Equity				
Current liabilities:				
Accounts payable	$ 67,000	$ 44,000	$ 23,000	52.3
Notes payable	3,000	6,000	(3,000)	(50.0)
Total current liabilities	$ 70,000	$ 50,000	$ 20,000	40.0
Long-term liabilities:				
Bonds payable, 8%	75,000	80,000	(5,000)	(6.3)
Total liabilities	$ 145,000	$ 130,000	$ 15,000	11.5
Shareholders' equity:				
Preferred stock	20,000	20,000	-	0.0
Common stock	60,000	60,000	-	0.0
Additional paid-in capital	10,000	10,000	-	0.0
Total paid-in capital	$ 90,000	$ 90,000	-	0.0
Retained earnings	80,000	69,700	10,300	14.8
Total shareholders' equity	$ 170,000	$ 159,700	$ 10,300	6.4
Total liabilities and shareholders' equity	$ 315,000	$ 289,700	$ 25,300	8.7

* Percent rounded to first decimal point.

Trend Analysis

Trend analysis is used to reveal patterns in data covering successive periods.

$$\text{Trend Percent} = \frac{\text{Analysis Period Amount}}{\text{Base Period Amount}} \times 100\%$$

Trend Analysis
Example

Berry Products
Income Information
For the Years Ended December 31,

Item	1998	1997	1996	1995	1994
Revenues	$ 400,000	$ 355,000	$ 320,000	$ 290,000	$ 275,000
Cost of sales	285,000	250,000	225,000	198,000	190,000
Gross profit	115,000	105,000	95,000	92,000	85,000

Item	1998	1997	1996	1995	1994
Revenues	145%	129%	116%		100%
Cost of sales	150%	132%	118%		100%
Gross profit	135%	124%	112%		100%

How would this trend analysis look on a line graph?

Trend Analysis
Example

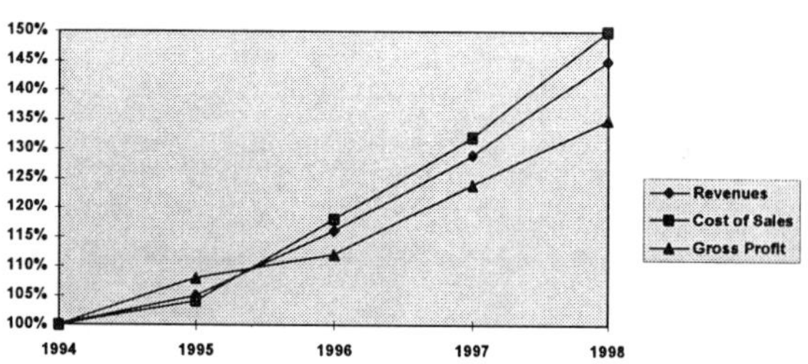

Common-Size Statements

Calculate Common-size Percent

$$\text{Common-size Percent} = \frac{\text{Analysis Amount}}{\text{Base Amount}} \times 100\%$$

Financial Statement	Base Amount
Balance Sheet	Total Assets
Income Statement	Revenues

CLOVER CORPORATION
Comparative Balance Sheets
December 31,

	1998	1997	Common-size Percents* 1998	Common-size Percents* 1997
Assets				
Current assets:				
Cash and equivalents	$ 12,000	$ 23,500	3.8%	8.1%
Accounts receivable, net	60,000	40,000	19.0%	13.8%
Inventory	80,000	100,000	25.4%	34.5%
Prepaid expenses	3,000	1,200	1.0%	0.4%
Total current assets	$ 155,000	$ 164,700	49.2%	56.9%
Property and equipment:				
Land	40,000	40,000	12.7%	13.8%
Buildings and equipment, net	120,000	85,000	38.1%	29.3%
Total property and equipment	$ 160,000	$ 125,000	50.8%	43.1%
Total assets	$ 315,000	$ 289,700	100.0%	100.0%

* Percent rounded to first decimal point.

CLOVER CORPORATION
Comparative Balance Sheets
December 31,

	1998	1997	Common-size Percents* 1998	Common-size Percents* 1997
Liabilities and Shareholders' Equity				
Current liabilities:				
Accounts payable	$ 67,000	$ 44,000	21.3%	15.2%
Notes payable	3,000	6,000	1.0%	2.1%
Total current liabilities	$ 70,000	$ 50,000	22.2%	17.3%
Long-term liabilities:				
Bonds payable, 8%	75,000	80,000	23.8%	27.6%
Total liabilities	$ 145,000	$ 130,000	46.0%	44.9%
Shareholders' equity:				
Preferred stock	20,000	20,000	6.3%	6.9%
Common stock	60,000	60,000	19.0%	20.7%
Additional paid-in capital	10,000	10,000	3.2%	3.5%
Total paid-in capital	$ 90,000	$ 90,000	28.6%	31.1%
Retained earnings	80,000	69,700	25.4%	24.1%
Total shareholders' equity	$ 170,000	$ 159,700	54.0%	55.1%
Total liabilities and shareholders' equity	$ 315,000	$ 289,700	100.0%	100.0%

* Percent rounded to first decimal point.

CLOVER CORPORATION Comparative Income Statements For the Years Ended December 31,				
			Common-size Percents*	
	1998	1997	1998	1997
Revenues	$520,000	$480,000	100.0%	100.0%
Costs and expenses:				
Cost of sales	360,000	315,000	69.2%	65.6%
Selling and admin.	128,600	126,000	24.7%	26.3%
Interest expense	6,400	7,000	1.2%	1.5%
Income before taxes	$ 25,000	$ 32,000	4.8%	6.7%
Income taxes (30%)	7,500	9,600	1.4%	2.0%
Net income	$ 17,500	$ 22,400	3.4%	4.7%
Net income per share	$ 0.79	$ 1.01		
Avg. # common shares	22,200	22,200		
* Rounded to first decimal point.				

Common-Size Graphics
Example

This is a graphical analysis of Clover Corporation's common-size income statement for 1998.

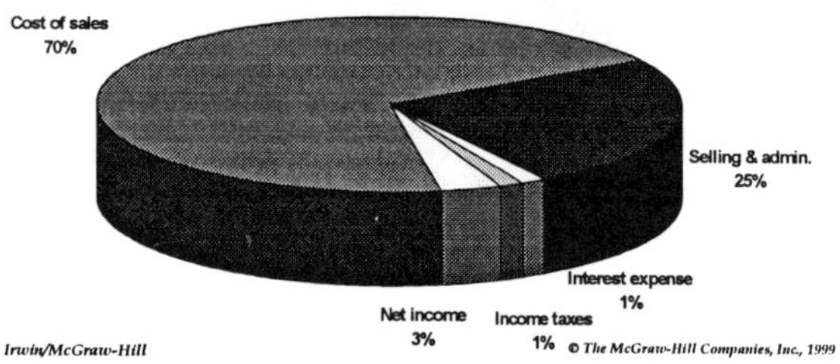

Irwin/McGraw-Hill

Common-Size Graphics
Example

This is a graphical analysis of Clover Corporation's common-size assets for 1998.

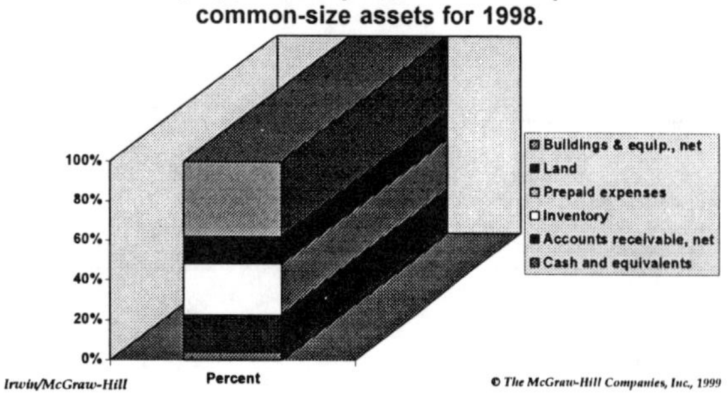

Irwin/McGraw-Hill

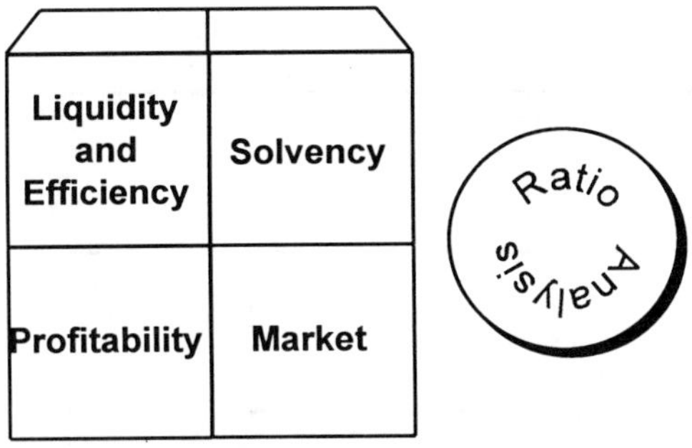

Let's use the following financial statements for Norton Corporation for our ratio analysis.

NORTON CORPORATION
Balance Sheet
December 31,

	1998	1997
Assets		
Current assets:		
Cash	$ 30,000	$ 20,000
Accounts receivable, net	20,000	17,000
Inventory	12,000	10,000
Prepaid expenses	3,000	2,000
Total current assets	$ 65,000	$ 49,000
Property and equipment:		
Land	165,000	123,000
Buildings and equipment, net	116,390	128,000
Total property and equipment	$ 281,390	$ 251,000
Total assets	$ 346,390	$ 300,000

NORTON CORPORATION
Balance Sheet
December 31,

	1998	1997
Liabilities and Shareholders' Equity		
Current liabilities:		
Accounts payable	$ 39,000	$ 40,000
Notes payable, short-term	3,000	2,000
Total current liabilities	$ 42,000	$ 42,000
Long-term liabilities:		
Notes payable, long-term	70,000	78,000
Total liabilities	$ 112,000	$ 120,000
Shareholders' equity:		
Common stock, $1 par value	27,400	17,000
Additional paid-in capital	158,100	113,000
Total paid-in capital	$ 185,500	$ 130,000
Retained earnings	48,890	50,000
Total shareholders' equity	$ 234,390	$ 180,000
Total liabilities and shareholders' equity	$ 346,390	$ 300,000

NORTON CORPORATION Income Statement For the Years Ended December 31,		
	1998	1997
Revenues	$ 494,000	$ 450,000
Cost of sales	140,000	127,000
Gross margin	$ 354,000	$ 323,000
Operating expenses	270,000	249,000
Net operating income	$ 84,000	$ 74,000
Interest expense	7,300	8,000
Net income before taxes	$ 76,700	$ 66,000
Less income taxes (30%)	23,010	19,800
Net income	$ 53,690	$ 46,200

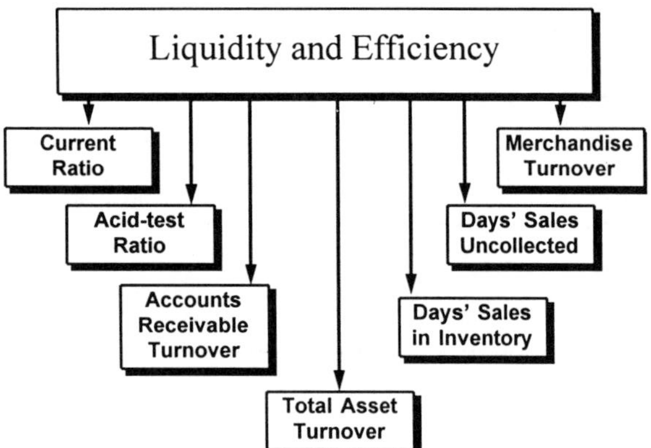

Use this information to calculate the liquidity and efficiency ratios for Norton Corporation.

NORTON CORPORATION 1998	
Cash	$ 30,000
Accounts receivable, net	
Beginning of year	17,000
End of year	20,000
Inventory	
Beginning of year	10,000
End of year	12,000
Total current assets	65,000
Total current liabilities	42,000
Total assets	
Beginning of year	300,000
End of year	346,390
Revenues	494,000
Cost of sales	140,000

Working Capital

Working capital represents current assets financed from long-term capital sources that do not require near-term repayment.

	Dec. 31, 1998
Current assets	$ 65,000
Current liabilities	(42,000)
Working capital	$ 23,000

Current Ratio

$$\text{Current Ratio} = \frac{\text{Current Assets}}{\text{Current Liabilities}}$$

$$\text{Current Ratio} = \frac{\$65,000}{\$42,000} = 1.55 : 1$$

This ratio measures the short-term debt-paying ability of the company.

Acid-Test Ratio

$$\text{Acid-Test Ratio} = \frac{\text{Quick Assets}}{\text{Current Liabilities}}$$

$$\text{Acid-Test Ratio} = \frac{\$50,000}{\$42,000} = 1.19 : 1$$

This ratio is like the current ratio but excludes current assets such as inventories that may be difficult to quickly convert into cash.

Accounts Receivable Turnover

$$\text{Accounts Receivable Turnover} = \frac{\text{Sales on Account}}{\text{Average Accounts Receivable}}$$

$$\text{Accounts Receivable Turnover} = \frac{\$494{,}000}{(\$17{,}000 + \$20{,}000) \div 2} = 26.7 \text{ times}$$

This ratio measures how many times a company converts its receivables into cash each year.

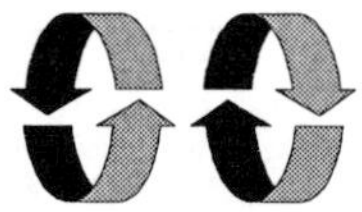

Merchandise Turnover

$$\text{Merchandise Turnover} = \frac{\text{Cost of Goods Sold}}{\text{Average Inventory}}$$

$$\text{Merchandise Turnover} = \frac{\$140{,}000}{(\$10{,}000 + \$12{,}000) \div 2} = 12.73 \text{ times}$$

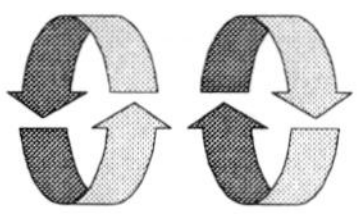

This ratio measures the number of times merchandise is sold and replaced during the year.

Days' Sales Uncollected

$$\text{Days' Sales Uncollected} = \frac{\text{Accounts Receivable}}{\text{Net Sales}} \times 365$$

$$\text{Days' Sales Uncollected} = \frac{\$20{,}000}{\$494{,}000} \times 365 = 14.8 \text{ days}$$

This ratio measures the liquidity of receivables.

Days' Sales in Inventory

$$\text{Days' Sales in Inventory} = \frac{\text{Ending Inventory}}{\text{Cost of Sales}} \times 365$$

$$\text{Days' Sales in Inventory} = \frac{\$12{,}000}{\$140{,}000} \times 365 = 31.29 \text{ days}$$

This ratio measures the liquidity of inventory.

Total Asset Turnover

$$\text{Total Asset Turnover} = \frac{\text{Revenues}}{\text{Average Total Assets}}$$

$$\text{Total Asset Turnover} = \frac{\$494{,}000}{(\$300{,}000 + \$346{,}390) \div 2} = 1.53 \text{ times}$$

This ratio measures the efficiency of assets in producing sales.

Solvency

- Debt Ratio
- Equity Ratio
- Pledged Assets to Secured Liabilities
- Times Interest Earned

Use this information to calculate the solvency ratios for Norton Corporation.

NORTON CORPORATION 1998	
Net income before interest expense and income taxes	$ 84,000
Interest expense	7,300
Total shareholders' equity	234,390
Total liabilities	112,000
Total assets	346,390

Debt Ratio

$$\text{Debt Ratio} = \frac{\text{Total Liabilities}}{\text{Total Assets}}$$

$$\text{Debt Ratio} = \frac{\$112{,}000}{\$346{,}390} = 32.3\%$$

This ratio measures what portion of a company's assets are contributed by creditors.

Equity Ratio

$$\text{Equity Ratio} = \frac{\text{Total Shareholders' Equity}}{\text{Total Assets}}$$

$$\text{Equity Ratio} = \frac{\$234{,}390}{\$346{,}390} = 67.7\%$$

This ratio measures what portion of a company's assets are contributed by owners.

Pledged Assets to Secured Liabilities

$$\text{Pledged Assets to Secured Liabilities} = \frac{\text{Book Value of Pledged Assets}}{\text{Book Value of Secured Liabilities}}$$

This ratio measures the protection to secured creditors.

Times Interest Earned

$$\text{Times Interest Earned} = \frac{\text{Net Income before Interest Expense and Income Taxes}}{\text{Interest Expense}}$$

$$\text{Times Interest Earned} = \frac{\$84,000}{\$7,300} = 11.51$$

This is the most common measure of the ability of a firm's operations to provide protection to the long-term creditor.

Profitability

- Profit Margin
- Gross Margin
- Return on Total Assets
- Return on Common Shareholders' Equity
- Book Value per Common Share
- Basic Earnings per Share

Use this information to calculate the profitability ratios for Norton Corporation.

NORTON CORPORATION 1998	
Number of common shares outstanding all of 1998	27,400
Net income	$ 53,690
Shareholders' equity	
Beginning of year	180,000
End of year	234,390
Revenues	494,000
Cost of sales	140,000
Total assets	
Beginning of year	300,000
End of year	346,390

Profit Margin

$$\text{Profit Margin} = \frac{\text{Net Income}}{\text{Net Sales}}$$

$$\text{Profit Margin} = \frac{\$53,690}{\$494,000} = 10.87\%$$

This ratio describes a company's ability to earn a net income from sales.

Gross Margin

$$\text{Gross Margin} = \frac{\text{Net Sales} - \text{Cost of Sales}}{\text{Net Sales}}$$

$$\text{Gross Margin} = \frac{\$494,000 - \$140,000}{\$494,000} = 71.66\%$$

This ratio measures the amount remaining from $1 in sales that is left to cover operating expenses and a profit after considering cost of sales.

Return on Total Assets

$$\text{Return on Total Assets} = \frac{\text{Net Income}}{\text{Average Total Assets}}$$

$$\text{Return on Total Assets} = \frac{\$53{,}690}{(\$300{,}000 + \$346{,}390) \div 2} = 16.61\%$$

This ratio is generally considered the best overall measure of a company's profitability.

Return on Common Shareholders' Equity

$$\text{Return on Common Shareholders' Equity} = \frac{\text{Net Income - Preferred Dividends}}{\text{Average Shareholders' Equity}}$$

$$\text{Return on Common Shareholders' Equity} = \frac{\$53{,}690 - 0}{(\$180{,}000 + \$234{,}390) \div 2} = 25.9\%$$

This measure indicates how well the company employed the owners' investments to earn income.

Book Value per Common Share

$$\text{Book Value per Common Share} = \frac{\text{Shareholders' Equity Applicable to Common Shares}}{\text{Number of Common Shares Outstanding}}$$

This ratio measures liquidation at reported amounts.

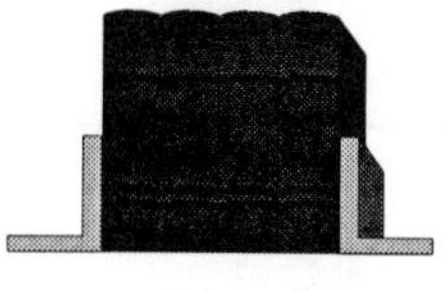

Basic Earnings per Share

$$\text{Basic Earnings per Share} = \frac{\text{Net Income - Preferred Dividends}}{\text{Weighted-Average Common Shares Outstanding}}$$

$$\text{Basic Earnings per Share} = \frac{\$53{,}690 - 0}{27{,}400} = \$1.96 \text{ per share}$$

This measure indicates how much income was earned for each share of common stock outstanding.

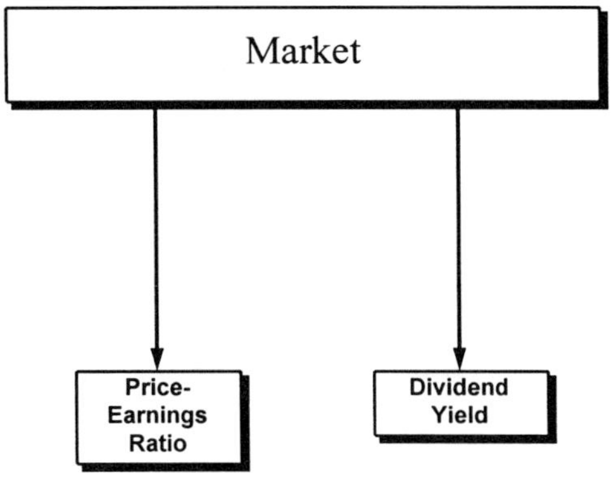

Use this information to calculate the market ratios for Norton Corporation.

NORTON CORPORATION December 31, 1998	
Earnings per Share	$ 1.96
Market Price	15.00
Annual Dividend per Share	2.00

Price-Earnings Ratio

$$\text{Price-Earnings Ratio} = \frac{\text{Market Price Per Share}}{\text{Earnings Per Share}}$$

$$\text{Price-Earnings Ratio} = \frac{\$15.00}{\$1.96} = 7.65 \text{ times}$$

This measure is often used by investors as a general guideline in gauging stock values. Generally, the higher the price-earnings ratio, the more opportunity a company has for growth.

Dividend Yield

$$\text{Dividend Yield} = \frac{\text{Annual Dividends Per Share}}{\text{Market Price Per Share}}$$

$$\text{Dividend Yield} = \frac{\$2.00}{\$15.00} = 13.3\%$$

This ratio identifies the return, in terms of cash dividends, on the current market price of the stock.

Analysis Reporting

❶Executive Summary

❷Analysis Overview

❸Evidential Matter

❹Assumptions

❺Important Factors

❻Inferences

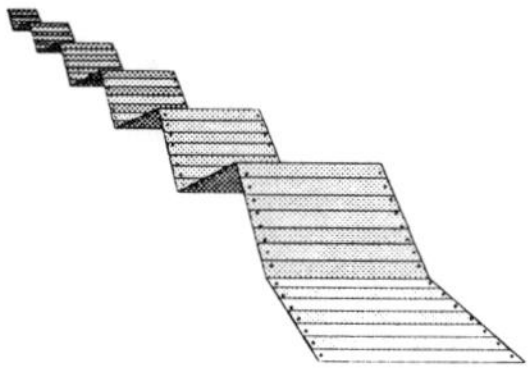

19 CHAPTER Managerial Accounting Concepts and Principles

Managerial and Financial Accounting

Managerial accounting provides information for managers of an organization who plan and control its operations.

Financial accounting provides information to stockholders, creditors and others who are outside the organization.

Planning and Control

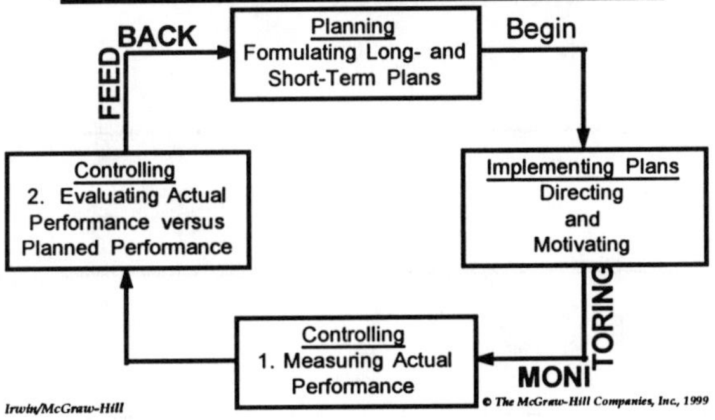

Nature of Managerial Accounting

Exh. 19-2

	Financial Accounting	Managerial Accounting
1. Users and decision makers	Investors, creditors and other external users	Managers, employees and other internal users
2. Purpose of information	Making investment, credit and other decisions	Planning, decision making and control
3. Flexibility of practice	Structured and often controlled by GAAP	Relatively flexible (no GAAP)
4. Timeliness of information	Often available only after audit is complete	Available quickly without need to wait for audit
5. Time dimension	Historical information with minimum predictions	Many projections and estimates
6. Focus of information	Emphasis on whole organization	Projects, processes and segments of an organization
7. Nature of information	Monetary information	Monetary and nonmonetary information

Irwin/McGraw-Hill

Reporting Manufacturing Activities

Merchandisers . . .

- ❖ Buy finished goods.
- ❖ Sell finished goods.

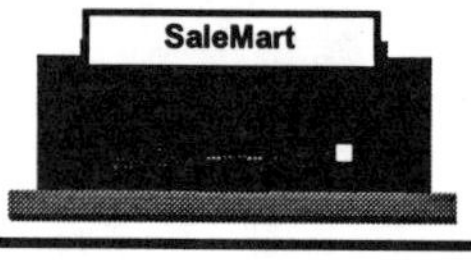

Manufacturers . . .

- ❖ Buy raw materials.
- ❖ Produce and sell finished goods.

Irwin/McGraw-Hill

Balance Sheet of a Manufacturer

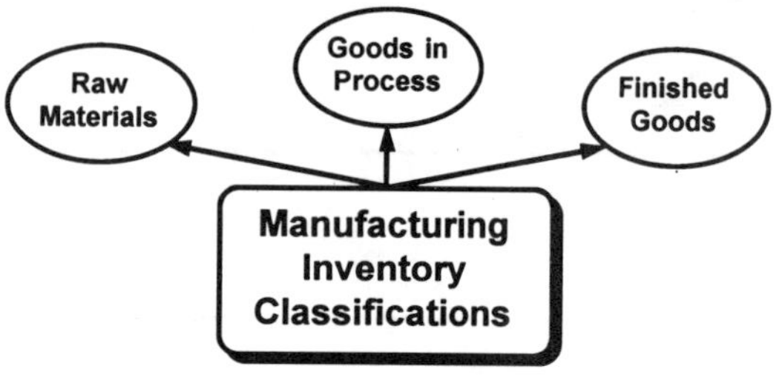

Irwin/McGraw-Hill

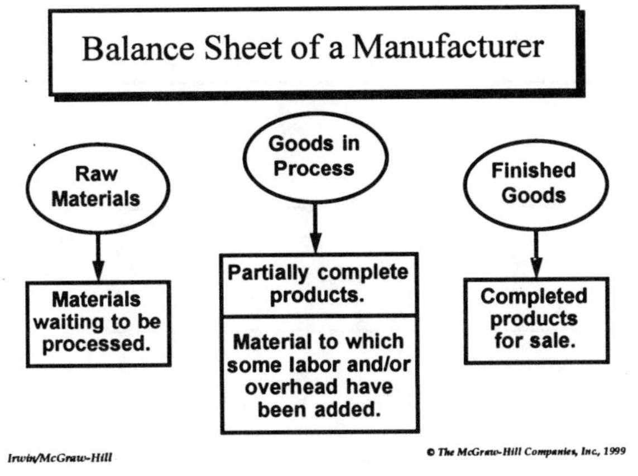
Balance Sheet of a Manufacturer
Raw Materials
Goods in Process
Finished Goods
Materials waiting to be processed.
Partially complete products.
Material to which some labor and/or overhead have been added.
Completed products for sale.
Irwin/McGraw-Hill
© The McGraw-Hill Companies, Inc, 1999

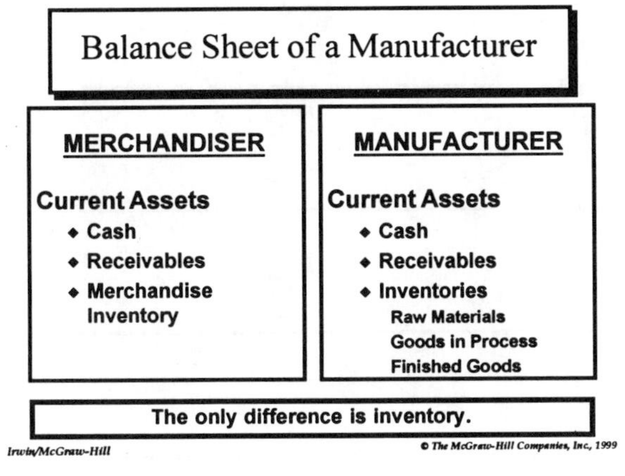
Balance Sheet of a Manufacturer
MERCHANDISER
Current Assets
◆ Cash
◆ Receivables
◆ Merchandise Inventory
MANUFACTURER
Current Assets
◆ Cash
◆ Receivables
◆ Inventories
Raw Materials
Goods in Process
Finished Goods
The only difference is inventory.
Irwin/McGraw-Hill
© The McGraw-Hill Companies, Inc, 1999

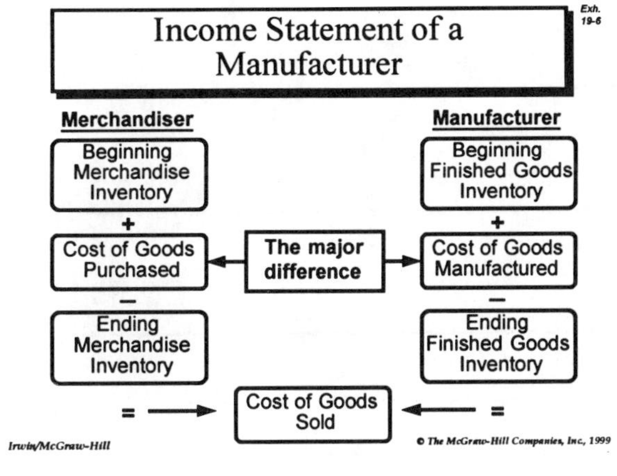
Income Statement of a Manufacturer
Exh. 19-6
Merchandiser
Beginning Merchandise Inventory
+
Cost of Goods Purchased
−
Ending Merchandise Inventory
=
The major difference
Manufacturer
Beginning Finished Goods Inventory
+
Cost of Goods Manufactured
−
Ending Finished Goods Inventory
=
Cost of Goods Sold
Irwin/McGraw-Hill
© The McGraw-Hill Companies, Inc, 1999

Income Statement of a Manufacturer

Exh. 19-7

Cost of goods sold for manufacturers differs only slightly from cost of goods sold for merchandisers.

Merchandising Company

Cost of goods sold:	
Beg. merchandise inventory	$ 14,200
+ Purchases	234,150
= Goods available for sale	$ 248,350
- Ending merchandise inventory	(12,100)
= Cost of goods sold	$ 236,250

Manufacturing Company

Cost of goods sold:	
Beg. finished goods inv.	$ 14,200
+ Cost of goods manufactured	234,150
= Goods available for sale	$ 248,350
- Ending finished goods inventory	(12,100)
= Cost of goods sold	$ 236,250

Income Statement of a Manufacturer

Direct Materials

Materials that are clearly and easily identified with a particular product.

Example:
Steel used to manufacture the automobile.

Income Statement of a Manufacturer

Direct Labor

Labor costs that are clearly traceable to, or readily identifiable with, the finished product.

Example:
Wages paid to an automobile assembly worker.

Income Statement of a Manufacturer

Factory Overhead

All factory costs except direct material and direct labor.

Factory costs that cannot be traced directly to specific units produced.

Examples:
Indirect labor – maintenance
Indirect material – cleaning supplies
Factory utility costs
Supervisory costs

Income Statement of a Manufacturer

Manufacturing costs are often combined as follows:

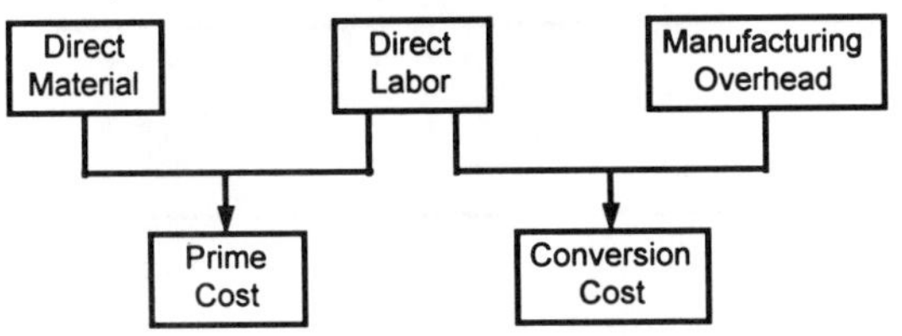

Question

What type of account is the manufacturing goods in process account?

a. Income statement expense account.
b. Balance sheet inventory account.
c. Temporary clearing account for direct material and direct labor.
d. Holding account for manufacturing overhead and direct labor.

Cost Accounting Concepts

- Behavior
- Traceability
- Controllability
- Relevance
- Function

Classification by Behavior

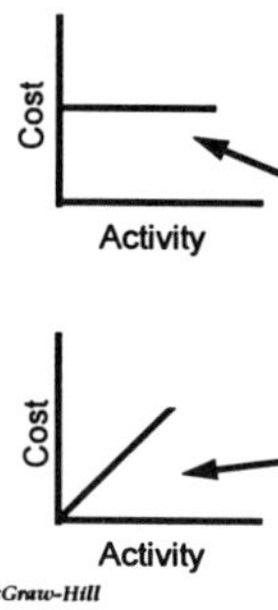

Cost behavior means how a cost will react to changes in the level of business activity.

- Total fixed costs do not change when activity changes.
- Total variable costs change in proportion to activity changes.

Classification by Traceability

Direct costs

- Costs that can be easily and conveniently traced to a unit of product or other cost objective.
- Examples: direct material and direct labor

Indirect costs

- Costs that must be allocated to a unit of product or other cost objective.
- Example: manufacturing overhead

Classification by Traceability

Direct material — Traced directly to one specific cost object → A product, process, department, or customer to which costs are assigned.

Direct labor — Traced directly to one specific cost object → A product, process, department, or customer to which costs are assigned.

Classification by Controllability

The degree of control depends on the level of management in the organization.

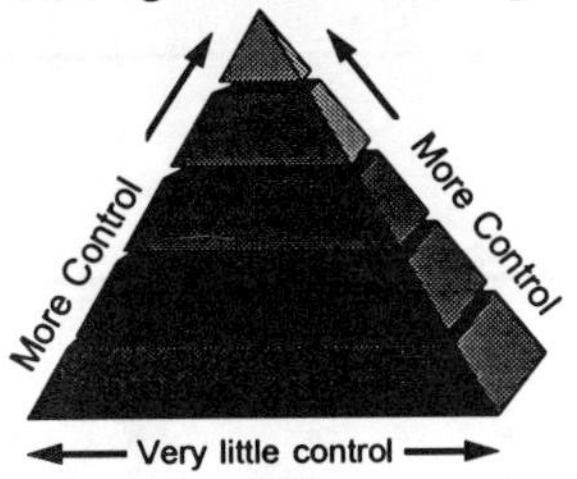

Classification by Relevance: Opportunity Costs

The potential benefit that is given up when one alternative is selected over another.

- Example: If you were not attending college, you could be earning $15,000 per year. Your opportunity cost of attending college for one year is $15,000.

Classification by Relevance: Sunk Costs

All costs incurred in the past that cannot be changed by any decision made now or in the future.

Sunk costs should not be considered in decisions.

Example: You bought an automobile that cost $10,000 two years ago. The $10,000 cost is sunk because whether you drive it, park it, trade it, or sell it, you cannot change the $10,000 cost.

Classification by Function: Product Costs

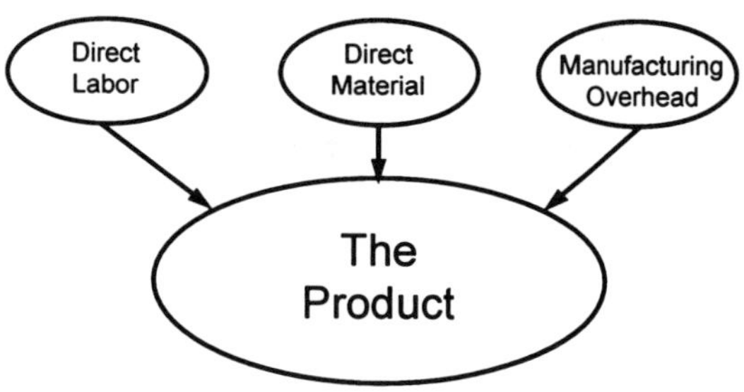

Classification by Function: Period Costs

Period costs are expenses not charged to the product.

Selling Costs

Costs incurred to obtain customer orders and to deliver finished goods to customers – advertising and shipping.

Administrative Costs

Nonmanufacturing costs of staff support and administrative functions – accounting, data processing, personnel, research and development.

Period and Product Costs in Financial Statements

Exh. 19-13

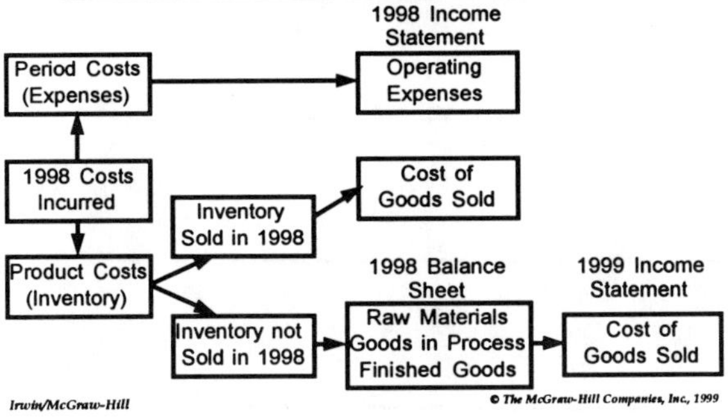

Question

The primary distinction between product and period costs is . . .

a. **Product costs are expensed in the period incurred.**
b. **Product costs are directly traceable to product units.**
c. **Product costs are inventoriable.**
d. **Period costs are inventoriable.**

Potential Multiple Cost Classifications

Exh. 19-14

Cost Item	Behavior	Traceability	Function
Material	Variable	Direct	Product
Assembly Wages	Variable	Direct	Product
Advertising	Fixed	Indirect	Period
Production Manager's Salary	Fixed	Indirect	Product
Office Depreciation	Fixed	Indirect	Period

Cost Concepts for Service Companies

Manufacturing Management Principles

Exh. 19-15

Total Quality Management

Quality throughout the production process.

Rewards for employees who find defects.

Employees encouraged to try new methods to improve quality.

Company emphasizes value of quality through quality awards.

Just-In-Time (JIT) Manufacturing

Receive customer orders.

↓

Schedule production.

↓

Receive materials just in time for production. → Complete parts just in time for assembly into products. → Complete products just in time to ship customers.

Theory of Constraints

A sequential process of identifying and removing constraints in a system.

Restrictions or barriers that impede progress toward an objective.

Continuous Improvement

New ways to improve operations

Implications of Manufacturing Management Principles

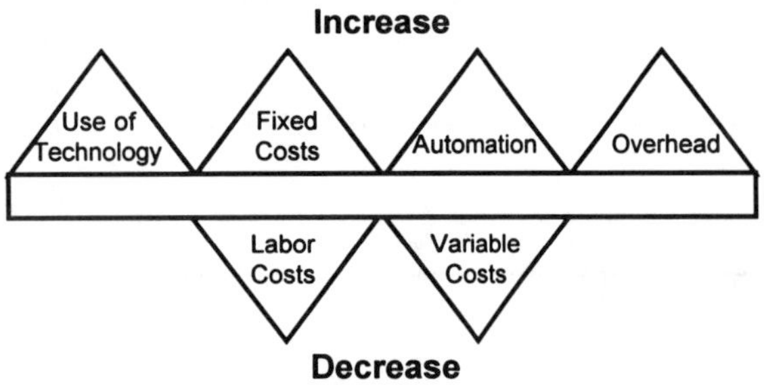

Unit Contribution Margin

	Total	Per Unit	Percent
Sales (500 units)	$ 250,000	$ 500	100%
Less: variable expenses	150,000	300	60%
Contribution margin	$ 100,000	$ 200	40%
Less: fixed expenses	80,000		
Net income	$ 20,000		

20 CHAPTER Manufacturing and Job Order Cost Accounting

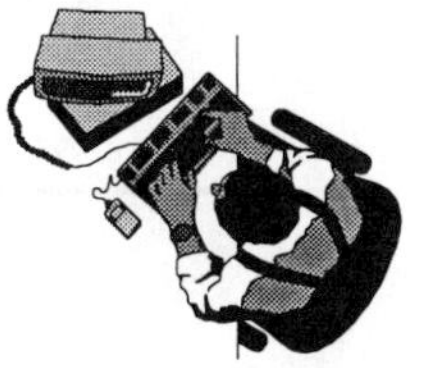

Irwin/McGraw-Hill

Flow of Manufacturing Activities

Exh. 20-1

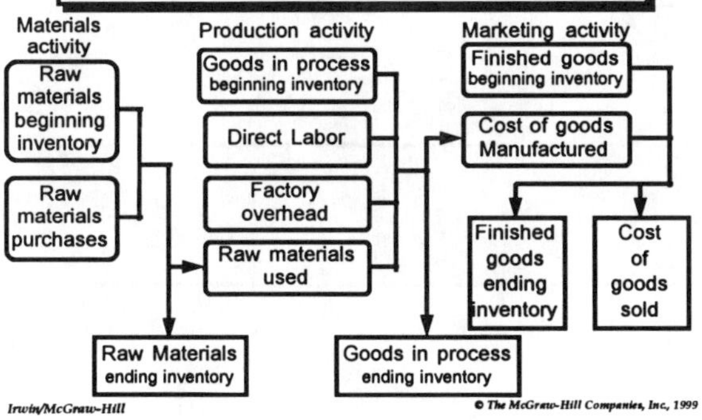

Irwin/McGraw-Hill

Manufacturing Statement

Cost of all goods completed and transferred from goods in process to finished goods during a reporting period.

	Direct Materials Used
+	Direct Labor
+	Manufacturing Overhead
=	Cost to Manufacture
+	Beginning Work in Process
–	Ending Work in Process
=	Cost of Goods Manufactured

Irwin/McGraw-Hill

Manufacturing Statement

Exh. 20-2

ROCKY MOUNTAIN BIKES Manufacturing Statement For Year Ended December 31,1998	
Direct materials used in production	$ 85,500
Direct labor	60,000
Total factory overhead costs	30,000
Total manufacturing costs for the period	$ 175,500
Add: Beginning goods in process inventory	2,500
Total cost of goods in process	$ 178,000
Deduct: Ending goods in process inventory	7,500
Cost of goods manufactured	$ 170,500

Exh. 20-2

Computation of Cost of Direct Material Used	
Beginning raw materials inventory	$ 8,000
Add: Purchases of raw materials	86,500
Cost of raw materials available for use	$ 94,500
Deduct: Ending raw materials inventory	9,000
Cost of direct materials used in production	$ 85,500

For Year Ended December 31,1998	
Direct materials used in production	$ 85,500
Direct labor	60,000
Total factory overhead costs	30,000
Total manufacturing costs for the period	$ 175,500
Add: Beginning goods in process inventory	2,500
Total cost of goods in process	$ 178,000
Deduct: Ending goods in process inventory	7,500
Cost of goods manufactured	$ 170,500

Exh. 20-2

Computation of Total Manufacturing Overhead	
Indirect labor	$ 9,000
Factory Supervision	6,000
Factory utilities	2,600
Property taxes, factory building	1,900
Factory supplies used	600
Factory insurance expired	1,100
Depreciation, building and equipment	5,300
Other factory overhead	3,500
Total factory overhead costs	$ 30,000

	$ 85,500
	60,000
Total factory overhead costs	30,000
Total manufacturing costs for the period	$ 175,500
Add: Beginning goods in process inventory	2,500
Total cost of goods in process	$ 178,000
Deduct: Ending goods in process inventory	7,500
Cost of goods manufactured	$ 170,500

Job Order Manufacturing

Process Costing | Job Costing

- Used for production of large, unique, high-cost items.
- Built to order rather than mass produced.
- Many costs can be directly traced to each job.

Job Order Manufacturing

Process Costing | Job Costing

- Typical job order cost applications:
  - Special-order printing
  - Building construction
- Also used in service industry
  - Hospitals
  - Law firms

Job Order Manufacturing

Process Costing | Job Costing

- Used for production of small, identical, low-cost items.
- Mass produced in automated continuous production process.
- Costs cannot be directly traced to each unit of product.

Job Order Manufacturing

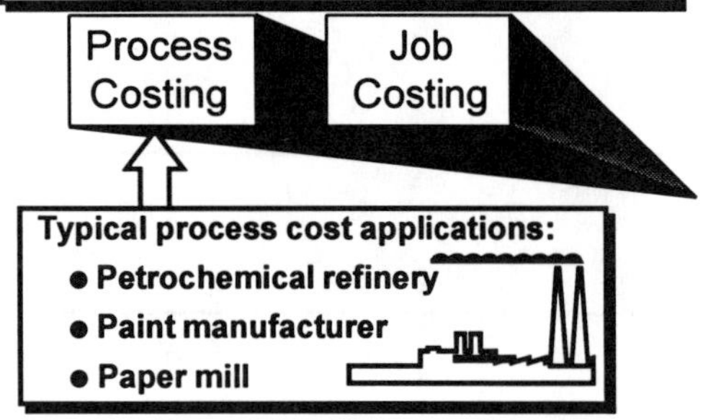

Events in Job Order Manufacturing

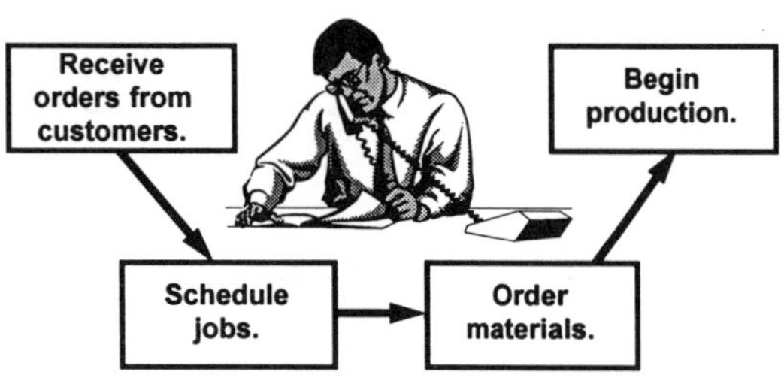

Job Order Manufacturing Activities

Exh. 20-3

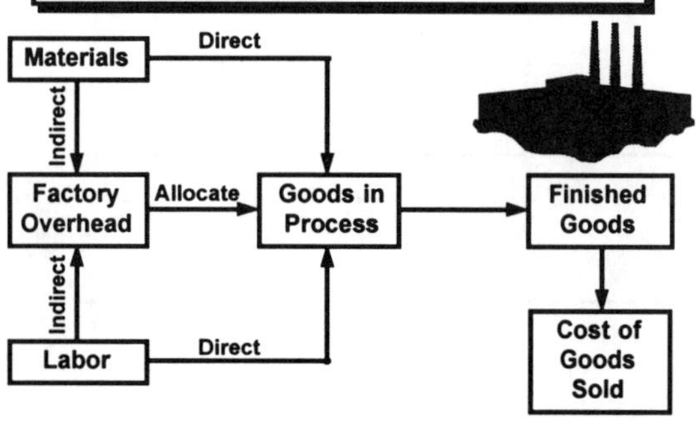

Job Cost Sheet

Exh. 20-4

Road Warriors Job Cost Sheet

Customer Carroll Connor Job No. B15
Address 1442 High Point Dr. Portland, Oregon
Job Description Level I Alarm System on Ford Expedition
Date promised 3/13 Dated started 3/3 Date completed

Direct Materials			Direct Labor			Factory Overhead		
Date	Req.	Cost	Date	Ticket	Cost	Date	Rate	Cost
Total			Total			Total		

Remarks	Cost Summary	
	Direct Materials	
	Direct Labor	
	Factory Overhead	
	Total Cost	

Materials Requisition

Exh. 20-7

Road Warriors Materials Requisition No. R-4705

Job No. B15 Date 3-7-98
Material Stock No. M-347
Material Description Alarm system wiring
Quantity Requested 1 Requested By C. Luther

Quantity Provided 1 Date Provided 3-7-98
Filled By M. Batemen Received By C. Luther
Remarks

Materials Ledger Card

Exh. 20-6

Road Warriors Materials Ledger Card

Item Alarm sys. wiring Stock No. M-347 Location Bin137
Maximum Qty. 5 units Minimum Qty. 1 unit Reorder Qty. 2 units

	Received				Issued				Balance		
Date	Rec. Rep.	Units	Unit Cost	Total Cost	Req. No.	Units	Unit Cost	Total Cost	Units	Unit Cost	Total Cost
									1	$225	$225
3/4/98	C7117	2	$225	$225					3	$225	$675
3/7/98					R4705	1	$225	$225	2	$225	$450

Exh. 20-4

Job Cost Sheet

Road Warriors Job Cost Sheet

Customer Carroll Connor Job No. B15
Address 1442 High Point Dr. Portland, Oregon
Job Description Level I Alarm System on Ford Expedition
Date promised 3/13 Dated started 3/3 Date completed

Direct Materials			Direct Labor			Factory Overhead		
Date	Req.	Cost	Date	Ticket	Cost	Date	Rate	Cost
3/7/98	R4705	$225						
Total		$225	Total			Total		

Remarks	Cost Summary	
	Direct Materials	$225
	Direct Labor	
	Factory Overhead	
	Total Cost	

Exh. 20-9

Labor Time Ticket

Road Warriors Time Ticket No. L-3479

Job No. B15 Date 3/8/98
Employee Name T. Zeller Employee Number 3969

TIME AND RATE INFORMATION:

Start Time 9:00 Finish Time 12:00
Elapsed Time 3.0 Hourly Rate $20.00 Total Cost $60.00
Approved By C. Luther
Remarks

Exh. 20-4

Job Cost Sheet

Road Warriors Job Cost Sheet

Customer Carroll Connor Job No. B15
Address 1442 High Point Dr. Portland, Oregon
Job Description Level I Alarm System on Ford Expedition
Date promised 3/13 Dated started 3/3 Date completed

Direct Materials			Direct Labor			Factory Overhead		
Date	Req.	Cost	Date	Ticket	Cost	Date	Rate	Cost
3/7/98	R4705	$225	3/8/98	L3479	$60			
Total		$225	Total		$60	Total		

Remarks	Cost Summary	
	Direct Materials	$225
	Direct Labor	60
	Factory Overhead	
	Total Cost	

Job Cost Sheet

Exh. 20-4

Road Warriors Job Cost Sheet

Customer Carroll Connor Job No. B15
Address 1442 High Point Dr. Portland, Oregon
Job Description Level I Alarm System on Ford Expedition
Date promised 3/13 Dated started 3/3 Date completed

Direct Materials			Direct Labor			Factory Overhead		
Date	Req.	Cost	Date	Ticket	Cost	Date	Rate	Cost
3/7/98	R4705	$225	3/8/98	L3479	$60	3/8/98	160%	$96
Total		$225	Total		$60	Total		$96

Remarks	Cost Summary	
	Direct Materials	$225
	Direct Labor	60
	Factory Overhead	96
	Total Cost	$381

Predetermined Overhead Allocation Rate Formula

Exh. 20-11

Road Warriors uses a predetermined overhead rate (POHR) based on direct labor cost to apply overhead to jobs.

$$\text{POHR} = \frac{\text{Estimated total manufacturing overhead cost for the coming period}}{\text{Estimated total direct labor costs for the coming period}}$$

$$\text{POHR} = \frac{\$200{,}000}{\$125{,}000} = 160\% \text{ of direct labor \$}$$

Job Order Costing Document Flow Summary

Exh. 20-5

The materials requisition indicates the cost of direct material to charge to jobs and the cost of indirect material to charge to overhead.

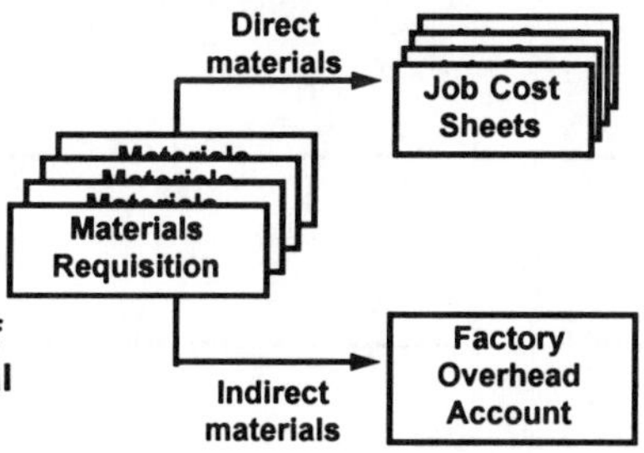

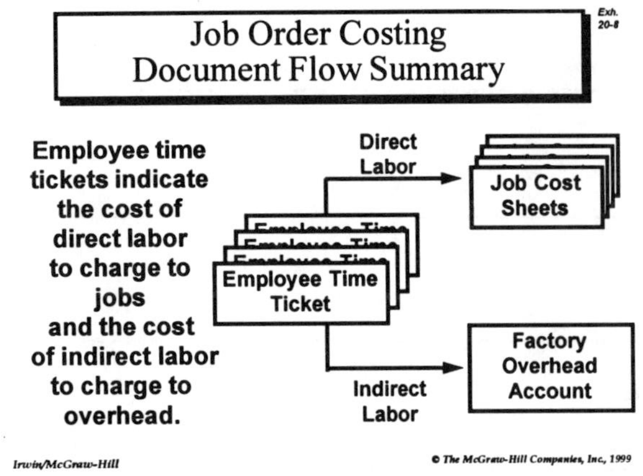
Job Order Costing
Document Flow Summary
Exh. 20-8
Employee time tickets indicate the cost of direct labor to charge to jobs and the cost of indirect labor to charge to overhead.
Direct Labor
Job Cost Sheets
Employee Time Ticket
Factory Overhead Account
Indirect Labor
Irwin/McGraw-Hill
© The McGraw-Hill Companies, Inc, 1999

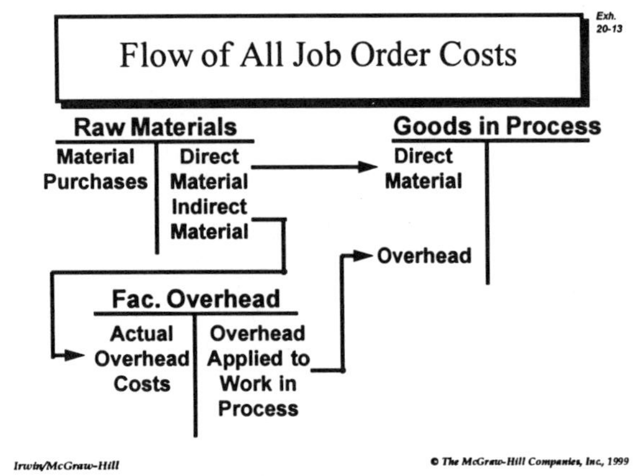
Flow of All Job Order Costs
Exh. 20-13
Raw Materials
Material Purchases
Direct Material
Indirect Material
Goods in Process
Direct Material
Overhead
Fac. Overhead
Actual Overhead Costs
Overhead Applied to Work in Process
Irwin/McGraw-Hill
© The McGraw-Hill Companies, Inc, 1999

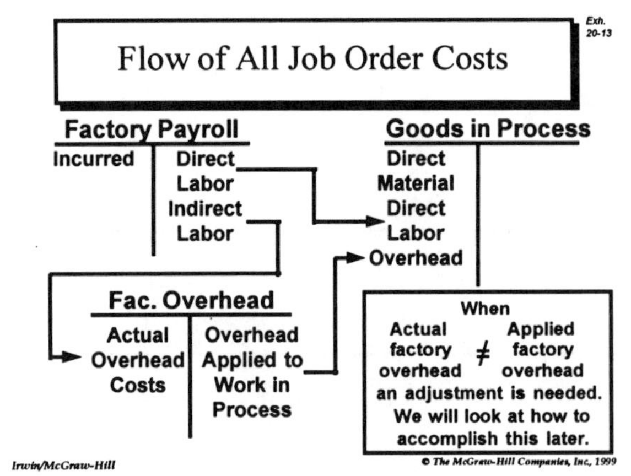
Flow of All Job Order Costs
Exh. 20-13
Factory Payroll
Incurred
Direct Labor
Indirect Labor
Goods in Process
Direct Material
Direct Labor
Overhead
Fac. Overhead
Actual Overhead Costs
Overhead Applied to Work in Process
When
Actual factory overhead ≠ Applied factory overhead
an adjustment is needed.
We will look at how to accomplish this later.
Irwin/McGraw-Hill
© The McGraw-Hill Companies, Inc, 1999

Flow of All Job Order Costs

Exh. 20-13

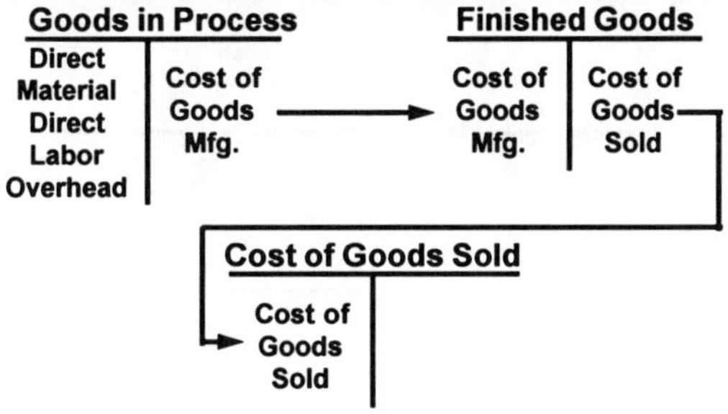

Overhead Application

Overhead Application

Question

If FishCo budgets overhead at $200,000 and estimates its activity to be 25,000 direct labor hours for 1999, what is the POHR per direct labor hour?

a. **$10.00 per hour**
b. **$ 6.00 per hour**
c. **$ 8.00 per hour**
d. **$12.00 per hour**

Question

If FishCo actually worked 24,000 direct labor hours for 1999, what amount of overhead would be assigned to jobs in work in process?

a. **$200,000**
b. **$192,000**
c. **$208,000**
d. **$196,000**

Overhead Application

Reasons for using a predetermined overhead rate

- Overhead is not incurred uniformly during the year.
- Actual overhead rate might vary from month to month.
- Predetermined rate makes it possible to estimate job costs sooner.

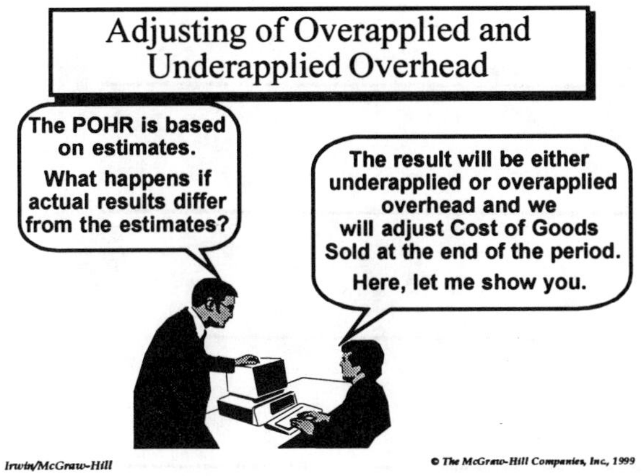
Adjusting of Overapplied and Underapplied Overhead
The POHR is based on estimates. What happens if actual results differ from the estimates?
The result will be either underapplied or overapplied overhead and we will adjust Cost of Goods Sold at the end of the period. Here, let me show you.
Irwin/McGraw-Hill
© The McGraw-Hill Companies, Inc, 1999

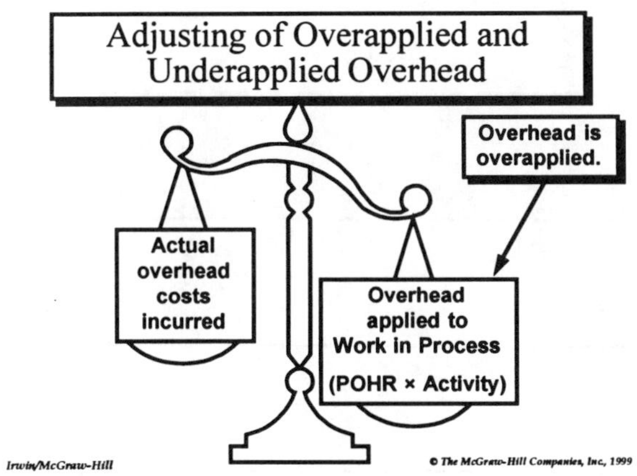
Adjusting of Overapplied and Underapplied Overhead
Overhead is overapplied.
Actual overhead costs incurred
Overhead applied to Work in Process (POHR × Activity)
Irwin/McGraw-Hill
© The McGraw-Hill Companies, Inc, 1999

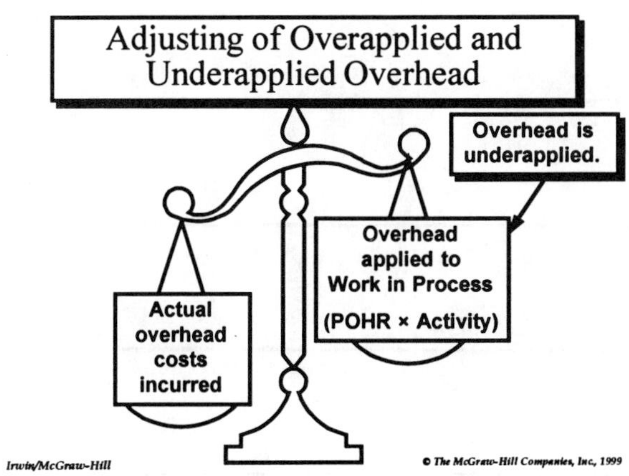
Adjusting of Overapplied and Underapplied Overhead
Overhead is underapplied.
Overhead applied to Work in Process (POHR × Activity)
Actual overhead costs incurred
Irwin/McGraw-Hill
© The McGraw-Hill Companies, Inc, 1999

Adjusting of Overapplied and Underapplied Overhead

Adjusting Cost of Goods Sold for underapplied or overapplied overhead

	Overhead is:	Cost of Goods Sold is:	Adjustment will:
Actual overhead > applied overhead	Underapplied	Too low	Increase Cost of Goods Sold
Actual overhead < applied overhead	Overapplied	Too high	Decrease Cost of Goods Sold

Question

FishCo had actual manufacturing overhead costs of $180,000. FishCo applied $192,000 of manufacturing overhead to jobs based on a POHR of $8.00 per direct labor hour. FishCo's manufacturing overhead is:

a. **$12,000 overapplied.**
b. **$12,000 underapplied.**
c. **$96,000 overapplied.**
d. **$96,000 underapplied.**

Question

The difference between FishCo's actual and applied overhead will result in an adjustment that decreases cost of goods sold.

a. **True**
b. **False**

21 CHAPTER Process Cost Accounting

Process Manufacturing Operations

- ✦ Used for production of small, identical, low-cost items.
- ✦ Mass produced in automated continuous production process.
- ✦ Costs cannot be directly traced to each unit of product.

Comparing Job Order and Process Production

Exh. 21-2

Job Order Systems	Process Systems
➢Custom orders	➢Repetitive production
➢Hetrogeneous products	➢Homogeneous products
➢Low production volume	➢High production volume
➢High product flexibility	➢Low product flexibility
➢Low to medium standardization	➢High standardization

Job Order and Process Cost Accounting

Exh. 21-7

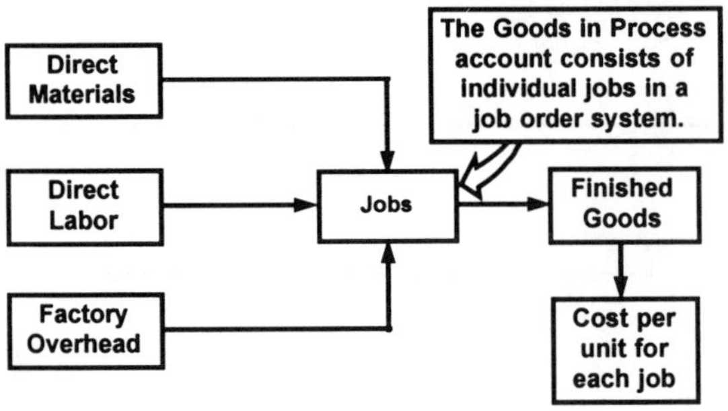

Job Order and Process Cost Accounting

Exh. 21-7

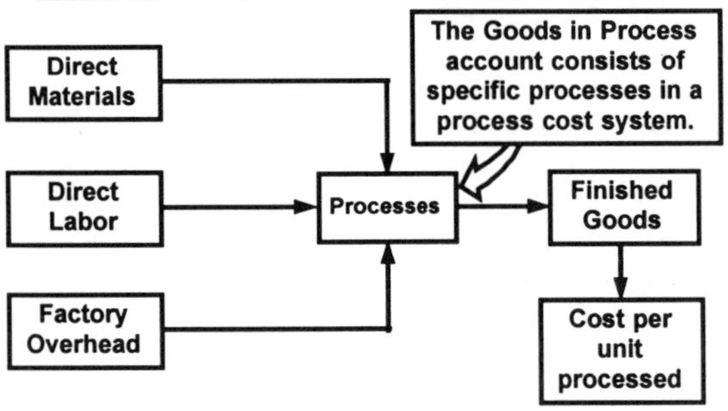

Job and Process Costing Similarities

- Same objective: to determine the cost of products
- Same inventory accounts: raw materials, work in process, and finished goods
- Same overhead assignment method: predetermined rate times actual activity

Computing and Using Equivalent Units of Production

Costs are accumulated for a period of time by process or department.

Unit cost is computed by dividing the accumulated costs by the number of equivalent units produced in the period.

Computing and Using Equivalent Units of Production

Equivalent units is a concept expressing a number of partially completed units as a smaller number of fully completed units.

Two one-half full pitchers are equivalent to one full pitcher.

Question

For the current period, PencilCo started 15,000 units and completed 10,000 units, leaving 5,000 units in process 30 percent complete. How many equivalent units of production did PencilCo have for the period?

a. **10,000**
b. **11,500**
c. **1,500**
d. **15,000**

Cost Per Equivalent Unit

$$\text{Cost per equivalent unit} = \frac{\text{Product costs for the period}}{\text{Equivalent units for the period}}$$

Question

Now assume that PencilCo incurred $27,600 in production costs. What was PencilCo's cost per unit for the period?

a. $1.84
b. $2.40
c. $2.76
d. $2.90

Equivalent Units

40% of Material	60% of Material	
↓	↓	
Stage 1	Stage 2	Stage 3
↑	↑	↑
25% of Labor and Overhead	25% of Labor and Overhead	50% of Labor and Overhead

The process is now complete.

Process Manufacturing Operations GenX

Exh. 21-6

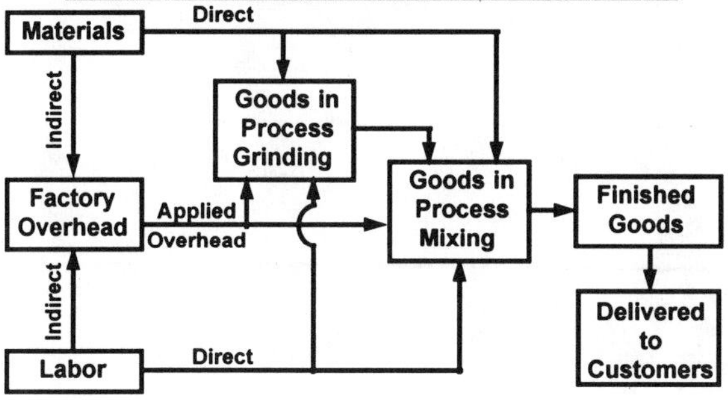

Accounting for GenX

Exh. 21-13

GenX Grinding Department Production Data April 1998	
Beginning Inventory:	
Units of product	30,000
Percentage of completion - direct materials	100%
Percentage of completion - direct labor	33 1/3%
Units started in April	90,000
Units transferred from grinding to mixing	100,000
Ending Inventory:	
Units of product	20,000
Percentage of completion - direct materials	100%
Percentage of completion - direct labor	25%

Accounting for GenX

Exh. 21-6

Manufacturing Costs During April 1998

	Raw Materials	Factory Payroll	Factory Overhead	Grinding	Mixing
Beginning balance	$ 4,000			$ 4,250	$ 3,520
Purchases and costs incurred	14,135	14,020	880		
Application of costs:					
Direct materials	(11,940)			9,900	2,040
Indirect materials	(1,195)		1,195		
Direct labor		(10,800)		5,700	5,100
Indirect labor		(3,220)	3,220		
Overhead applied			(5,295)	4,275	1,020

Accounting for GenX

GenX uses a FIFO cost flow system with the following four steps:

❶ Physical flow of units.
❷ Computing equivalent units of production.
❸ Computing cost per equivalent unit.
❹ Cost reconciliation.

Exh. 21-14

❶ Physical Flow of Units

GenX Grinding Department Physical Flow April 1998

Units to account for:	
Beginning inventory	30,000
Units started during April	90,000
Total number of units	120,000
Units accounted for as:	
Units transferred from grinding to mixing	100,000
Ending inventory	20,000
Total number of units	120,000

Exh. 21-15

❷ Computing Equivalent Units of Production

GenX Grinding Department
Direct Materials Equivalent Units of Production - April 1998

	Units of Product	Percent Added This Period	Equivalent Units
Beginning goods in process	30,000	0%	0
Goods started and completed	70,000	100%	70,000
Ending goods in process	20,000	100%	20,000
Total units	120,000		120,000

❷ Computing Equivalent Units of Production

Exh. 21-16

GenX Grinding Department Direct Labor and Factory Overhead Equivalent Units of Production - April 1998	Units of Product	Percent Added This Period	Equivalent Units
Beginning goods in process	30,000	66 2/3%	20,000
Goods started and completed	70,000	100%	70,000
Ending goods in process	20,000	25%	5,000
Total units	120,000		95,000

❷ Computing Equivalent Units of Production

Exh. 21-17

GenX Grinding Department
Equivalent Units of Production - April 1998

Activities during April 1998	Direct Materials	Direct Labor	Factory Overhead
Units from beginning inventory processed in current period	0	20,000	20,000
Units started and completed in current period	70,000	70,000	70,000
Units in ending inventory at end of current period	20,000	5,000	5,000
Equivalent units of production for period	90,000	95,000	95,000

❸ Cost per Equivalent Unit

Exh. 21-18

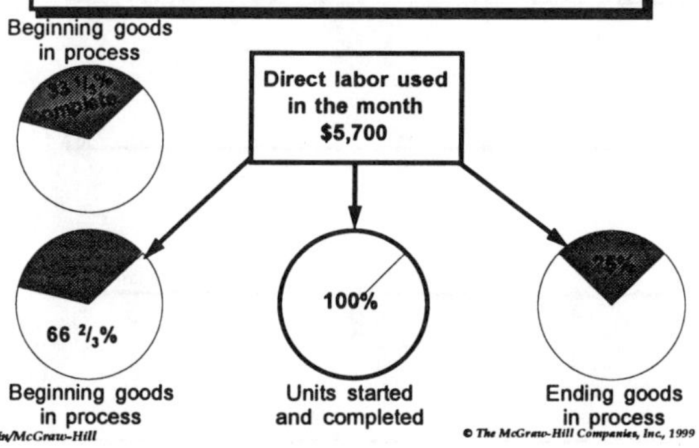

Exh. 21-19

❸ Cost per Equivalent Unit

GenX Grinding Department
Cost Per Equivalent Unit - April 1998

Activities during April 1998	Direct Materials	Direct Labor	Factory Overhead
Costs assigned to grinding in the current period	$ 9,900	$ 5,700	$ 4,275
Equivalent units of production in the current period	÷ 90,000	÷ 95,000	÷ 95,000
Cost per equivalent unit for the current period	= $ 0.11	= $ 0.06	= $ 0.045

❹ Cost Reconciliation

In the cost reconciliation, we will account for all costs incurred by assigning unit costs to the:

A. 100,000 units transferred from grinding to mixing.

B. 20,000 units remaining in ending inventory.

Exh. 21-20

GenX Grinding Department
Cost Reconciliation - April 1998

Costs to Account for:	
From Beginning Inventory	$ 4,250
Assigned in April 1998	
(Direct materials, direct labor and factory overhead)	19,875
Total costs to account for	$ 24,125
Costs Accounted for as:	
Beginning inventory completed in April 1998:	
Costs from previous period	4,250
Costs assigned during current period:	
Direct materials (0 units @ $0.11)	0
Direct labor (20,000 units @ $0.06)	1,200
Factory overhead (20,000 units @ $0.045)	900
Total costs to process beginning inventory in current period	$ 6,350
Cost of units started and completed in April 1998 (70,000 units @ $0.215)	$ 15,050
Units in ending inventory	
Direct materials (20,000 units @ $0.11)	2,200
Direct labor (5,000 units @ $0.06)	300
Factory overhead (5,000 units @ $0.045)	225
Total costs of units in ending inventory	$ 2,725
Total costs accounted for	$ 24,125

Process Cost Summary

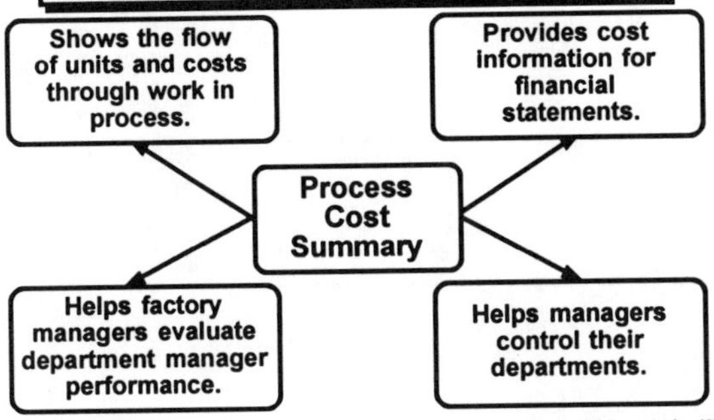

Process Cost Summary

We will illustrate the process cost summary for the Grinding Department of GenX in three sections:

- **Costs charged to department.**
- **Equivalent unit processing costs.**
- **Assignment of costs to output of department.**

Process Cost Summary

Exh. 21-21

GenX Company Grinding Department
Process Cost Summary for Grinding Department
For the Month Ended April 30, 1998

COSTS CHARGED TO DEPARTMENT

Direct materials requisitioned	$ 9,900
Direct labor charged	5,700
Overhead allocated (at predetermined rate)	4,275
Total processing costs for the month	$ 19,875
Goods in process at the beginning of the month	4,250
Total costs to be accounted for	**$ 24,125**

GenX Company Grinding Department
Process Cost Summary for Grinding Department
For the Month Ended April 30, 1998

Exh. 21-21

EQUIVALENT UNIT PROCESSING COSTS

	Units of Product	Equivalent Units: Direct Materials	Equivalent Units: Labor and Overhead
Units processed			
Beginning goods in process	30,000	-	20,000
Units started and completed	70,000	70,000	70,000
Ending goods in process	20,000	20,000	5,000
Total	120,000	90,000	95,000
Total direct materials for April			$ 9,900
Direct materials cost per equivalent unit ($9,900/90,000 units)			$ 0.110
Total direct labor cost for April			$ 5,700
Direct labor cost per equivalent unit ($5,700/95,000 units)			$ 0.060
Total factory overhead cost for April			$ 4,275
Factory overhead cost per equivalent unit ($4,275/95,000 units)			$ 0.045

GenX Company Grinding Department
Process Cost Summary for Grinding Department
For the Month Ended April 30, 1998

Exh. 21-21

ASSIGNMENT OF COSTS TO OUTPUT OF DEPARTMENT

	Equivalent Units	Cost per Unit	Total Cost
Goods in process, March 31 and completed during April:			
Costs from prior month			$ 4,250
Direct materials added (none)			0
Direct labor added	20,000	$ 0.060	1,200
Factory overhead added	20,000	0.045	900
Total costs to process			$ 6,350
Goods started and completed during April:			
Direct materials added	70,000	0.110	7,700
Direct labor added	70,000	0.060	4,200
Factory overhead added	70,000	0.045	3,150
Total costs to process		0.2150	$15,050
Total costs transferred to mixing (100,000 units @ $0.214)			$21,400
Goods in process, April 30, 1998			
Direct materials added	20,000	0.110	2,200
Direct labor added	5,000	0.060	300
Factory overhead added	5,000	0.045	225
Total costs to process		0.2150	$ 2,725
Total costs accounted for			$24,125

Accounting for GenX

Exh. 21-23

GenX Mixing Department Production Data April 1998

Beginning inventory:	
Units of product	16,000
Percentage of completion	25%
Units received from grinding department	100,000
Units transferred to finished goods	101,000
Ending Inventory:	
Units of product	15,000
Percentage of completion	33 1/3%

GenX Mixing Department Equivalent Units of Production

Exh. 21-24

GenX Mixing Department
Equivalent Unit of Production

	Units of Product	Percent Added	Equivalent Units
Beginning goods in process	16,000	75%	12,000
Goods started and completed	85,000	100%	85,000
Ending goods in process	15,000	33 1/3%	5,000
Total Units	116,000		102,000

Process Cost Summary

Exh. 21-25

GenX Company Mixing Department
Process Cost Summary for Mixing Department
For the Month Ended April 30, 1998

COSTS CHARGED TO DEPARTMENT	
Direct materials requisitioned	$ 2,040
Direct labor charged	5,100
Overhead allocated (at predetermined rate)	1,020
Total processing costs for the month	$ 8,160
Goods in process at the beginning of the month	3,520
Costs transferred in from grinding department	21,400
Total costs to be accounted for	$ 33,080

Exh. 21-25

GenX Company Mixing Department
Process Cost Summary for Mixing Department
For the Month Ended April 30, 1998

EQUIVALENT UNIT PROCESSING COSTS

	Units of Product	Equivalent Units of Production
Units processed		
Beginning goods in process	16,000	12,000
Units started and completed	85,000	85,000
Ending goods in process	15,000	5,000
Total	116,000	102,000
Total direct materials for April		$ 2,040
Direct materials cost per equivalent unit ($2,040/102,000 units)		$ 0.020
Total direct labor cost for April		$ 5,100
Direct labor cost per equivalent unit ($5,100/102,000 units)		$ 0.050
Total factory overhead cost for April		$ 1,020
Factory overhead cost per equivalent unit ($1,020/102,000 units)		$ 0.010

GenX Company Mixing Department
Process Cost Summary for Mixing Department
For the Month Ended April 30, 1998

Exh. 21-25

ASSIGNMENT OF COSTS TO OUTPUT OF DEPARTMENT

	Equivalent Units	Cost per Unit	Total Cost
Goods in process, March 31 and completed during April:			
Costs from prior month			$ 3,520
Direct materials added (none)	12,000	$ 0.020	240
Direct labor added	12,000	$ 0.050	600
Factory overhead added	12,000	$ 0.010	120
Total costs to process			$ 4,480
Goods started and completed during April:			
Costs transferred in (85,000 × $0.214)			$ 18,190
Direct materials added	85,000	$ 0.020	1,700
Direct labor added	85,000	$ 0.050	4,250
Factory overhead added	85,000	$ 0.010	850
Total costs to process			$ 24,990
Total costs transferred to finished goods			$ 29,470
Goods in process, April 30, 1998			
Costs transferred in (15,000 × $0.214)			$ 3,210
Direct materials added	5,000	$ 0.020	100
Direct labor added	5,000	$ 0.050	250
Factory overhead added	5,000	$ 0.010	50
Total costs to process			$ 3,610
Total costs accounted for			$ 33,080

Spoiled Units

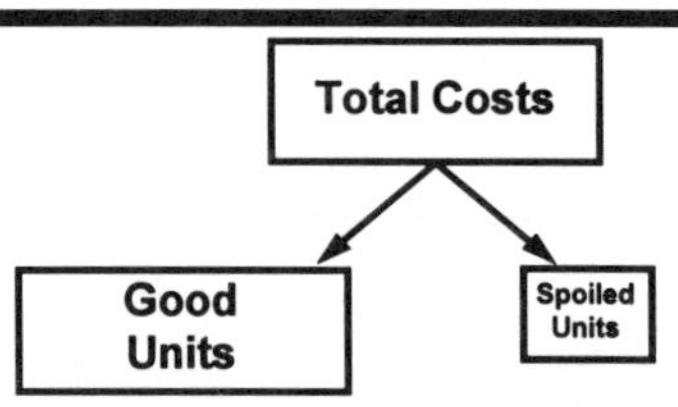

Assigning costs to spoiled units alerts managment to spoilage costs and avoids overstating the cost of good units.

Example

Irwin/McGraw-Hill

Spoiled Units

Exh. 21-30

	Equivalent Units	Production Costs
Good units	900	
Spoiled units	100	
Total	1,000	$ 18,000

Cost per equivalent unit:

Spoiled units ignored	$18,000 ÷ 900 units = $20 per unit
Total costs assigned:	
To good units	900 units × $20 = $18,000
To spoiled units	$0
Spoilage included	$18,000 ÷ 1000 units = $18 per unit
Total costs assigned:	
To good units	900 units × $18 = $16,200
To spoiled units	100 units × $18 = $1,800

Irwin/McGraw-Hill

Process Costing
Typical Accounting Entries

GENERAL JOURNAL — Page 21

Date		Description	Post. Ref.	Debit	Credit
		Raw Materials Inventory		XXXXX	
		Accounts Payable			XXXXX
		Acquired materials on credit for			
		use in the factory.			

Process Costing
Typical Accounting Entries

GENERAL JOURNAL — Page 21

Date		Description	Post. Ref.	Debit	Credit
		Goods in Process Inv. - Grinding		XXXXX	
		Goods in Process Inv. - Mixing		XXXXX	
		Raw Materials Inventory			XXXXX
		To assign costs of direct material			
		used in the grinding and mixing			
		departments.			

Process Costing
Typical Accounting Entries

GENERAL JOURNAL — Page 21

Date		Description	Post. Ref.	Debit	Credit
		Factory Overhead		XXXXX	
		Raw Materials Inventory			XXXXX
		To record indirect materials used			
		in April.			

Process Costing
Typical Accounting Entries

GENERAL JOURNAL				Page 21	
Date		Description	Post. Ref.	Debit	Credit
		Factory Payroll		XXXXX	
		Cash			XXXXX
		To record factory wages for April.			

Process Costing
Typical Accounting Entries

GENERAL JOURNAL				Page 21	
Date		Description	Post. Ref.	Debit	Credit
		Goods in Process Inv. - Grinding		XXXXX	
		Goods in Process Inv. - Mixing		XXXXX	
		Factory Payroll			XXXXX
		To assign costs of direct labor			
		used in the grinding and mixing			
		departments.			

Process Costing
Typical Accounting Entries

GENERAL JOURNAL				Page 21	
Date		Description	Post. Ref.	Debit	Credit
		Factory Overhead		XXXXX	
		Factory Payroll			XXXXX
		To record indirect labor as			
		overhead.			

Process Costing
Typical Accounting Entries

GENERAL JOURNAL			Page 21		
Date		Description	Post. Ref.	Debit	Credit
		Factory Overhead		XXXXX	
		Prepaid Insurance			XXXXX
		Accrued Utilities Payable			XXXXX
		Cash			XXXXX
		Accumulated Depreciation			XXXXX
		To record factory overhead items			
		incurred during April.			

Process Costing
Typical Accounting Entries

GENERAL JOURNAL			Page 21		
Date		Description	Post. Ref.	Debit	Credit
		Goods in Process Inv. - Grinding		XXXXX	
		Goods in Process Inv. - Mixing		XXXXX	
		Factory Overhead			XXXXX
		Allocated factory overhead costs to			
		the grinding department and to the			
		mixing department on the basis of			
		direct labor cost.			

Process Costing
Typical Accounting Entries

GENERAL JOURNAL			Page 21		
Date		Description	Post. Ref.	Debit	Credit
		Goods in Process Inv. - Mixing		XXXXX	
		Goods in Process Inv. - Grinding			XXXXX
		To record the transfer of partially			
		completed goods from the grinding			
		department to the mixing			
		department.			

Process Costing
Typical Accounting Entries

GENERAL JOURNAL				Page 21	
Date		Description	Post. Ref.	Debit	Credit
		Finished Goods Inventory		XXXXX	
		Goods in Process Inv. - Mixing			XXXXX
		To record the transfer of completed			
		goods out of production.			

Process Costing
Typical Accounting Entries

GENERAL JOURNAL				Page 21	
Date		Description	Post. Ref.	Debit	Credit
		Cost of Goods Sold		XXXXX	
		Finished Goods Inventory			XXXXX
		To record cost of goods sold			
		during April.			

22 CHAPTER Cost Allocation and Performance Measurement

Additional Methods of Overhead Cost Allocation

One of the most difficult tasks in computing accurate unit costs lies in determining the proper amount of overhead cost to assign to each job.

Additional Methods of Overhead Cost Allocation

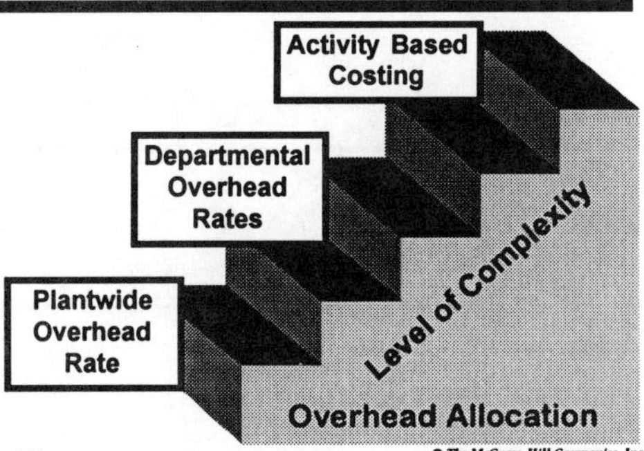

Two-Stage Cost Allocation

A two-stage process may be used because different departments may have different allocation bases.

Two-Stage Cost Allocation

Stage One:
Costs assigned to departments

Stage Two:
Costs applied to jobs

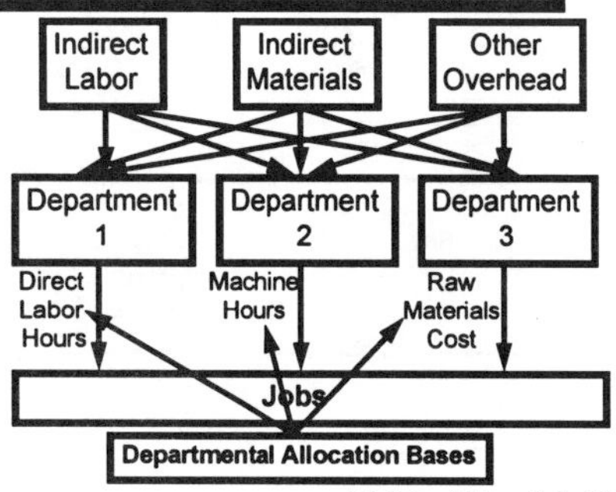

Activity-Based Costing

In the ABC method, we recognize that many activities within a department drive overhead costs.

Activity-Based Costing

Identify activities and assign indirect costs to those activities.

Central idea . . .

- Products require activities.
- Activities consume resources.

Activity-Based Costing
Benefits

- ➢ More detailed measures of costs.
- ➢ Better understanding of activities.
- ➢ More accurate product costs for . . .
  - Pricing decisions.
  - Product elimination decisions.
  - Managing activities that cause costs.
- ➢ Benefits should always be compared to costs of implementation.

Identifying Cost Drivers

Most cost drivers are related to either volume or complexity of production.

- Examples: machine time, machine setups, purchase orders, production orders.

Three factors are considered in choosing a cost driver:

- Causal relationship.
- Benefits received.
- Reasonableness.

Activity-Based Costing
Procedures

❶ Identify activities that consume resources.

❷ Assign costs to a cost pool for each activity.

❸ Identify cost drivers associated with each activity.

❹ Compute overhead rate for each cost pool:

$$\text{Rate} = \frac{\text{Estimated overhead costs in activity cost pool}}{\text{Estimated number of activity units}}$$

❺ Assign costs to products:

$$\text{Overhead Rate} \times \text{Actual Activity}$$

Traditional Costing vs. ABC
Example

Pear Company manufactures a product in regular and deluxe models. Overhead is assigned on the basis of direct labor hours. Budgeted overhead for the current year is $2,000,000. Other information:

	Deluxe Model	Regular Model
Direct Material	$ 150	$ 112
Direct Labor Cost	16	8
Direct Labor Time	1.6 hours	0.8 hours
Expected Volume (units)	5,000	40,000

First, determine the unit cost of each model using traditional costing methods.

Traditional Costing

		Direct Labor Hours
Deluxe Model	5,000 units @ 1.6 hours	8,000
Regular Model	40,000 units @ 0.8 hours	32,000
Total Direct Labor Hours (DLH)		40,000

$$\text{Overhead Rate} = \frac{\text{Estimated overhead costs}}{\text{Estimated activity}}$$

$$\text{Overhead Rate} = \frac{\$2,000,000}{40,000\ \text{DLH}} = \$50 \text{ per DLH}$$

Traditional Costing

ABC will have different overhead per unit.

	Deluxe Model	Regular Model
Direct Material	$ 150	$ 112
Direct Labor	16	8
Manufacturing Overhead		
$50 per hour × 1.6 hours	80	
$50 per hour × 0.8 hours		40
Total Unit Cost	$ 246	$ 160

Activity-Based Costing

Pear Company plans to adopt activity-based costing. Using the following activity center data, determine the unit cost of the two products using activity-based costing.

Activity Center	Cost Driver	Overhead Cost for Activity	Units of Activity Deluxe	Units of Activity Regular
Purchasing	Orders	$ 84,000	400	800
Scrap Rework	Orders	216,000	300	600
Testing	Tests	450,000	4,000	11,000
Machine Related	Hours	1,250,000	20,000	30,000
Total Overhead		$2,000,000		

Activity-Based Costing

Activity Center	Cost Driver	Overhead Cost for Activity	Units of Activity	Rate
Purchasing	Orders	$ 84,000	1,200	$ 70 per order
Scrap Rework	Orders	216,000	900	$240 per order
Testing	Tests	450,000	15,000	$ 30 per test
Machine Related	Hours	1,250,000	50,000	$ 25 per hour
Total Overhead		$2,000,000		

Rate = Overhead Cost for Activity ÷ Units of Activity

Activity-Based Costing

Activity	Rate	Deluxe Model: Actual Units of Activity	Deluxe Model: Cost Allocated to Product	Regular Model: Actual Units of Activity	Regular Model: Cost Allocated to Product
Purchasing	$ 70/order	400	$ 28,000	800	$ 56,000
Scrap Rework	$240/order	300	?	600	?
Testing	$ 30/test	4,000	?	11,000	?
Machine Related	$ 25/hour	20,000	?	30,000	?
Total overhead			?		?

Cost Allocated to Product = Actual Units of Activity × Rate

Let's complete the table.

Activity-Based Costing

Overhead Costs Assigned to Products:

Deluxe Model $720,000 ÷ 5,000 units = $144 per unit

Regular Model $1,280,000 ÷ 40,000 units = $32 per unit

	Deluxe Model	Regular Model
Direct Materials	$ 150	$ 112
Direct Labor	16	8
Manufacturing Overhead	144	32
Total Unit Cost	$ 310	$ 152

Traditional Costing vs. ABC

	Traditional Costing: Deluxe Model	Traditional Costing: Regular Model	ABC: Deluxe Model	ABC: Regular Model
Direct labor	$ 150	$ 112	$ 150	$ 112
Direct material	16	8	16	8
Overhead	80	40	144	32
Total cost	$ 246	$ 160	$ 310	$ 152

This result is not uncommon when activity-based costing is used. Many companies have found that low-volume, specialized products have greater overhead costs than previously realized.

Costs and Cost Drivers in Activity-Based Costing

Exh. 22-6

Cost	Cost Driver
Materials purchasing	Number of purchase orders
Materials handling	Number of materials requisitions
Personnel processing	Number of employees hired or laid off
Equipment depreciation	Number of products produced or hours of use
Quality Inspection	Number of units inspected
Indirect labor for equipment setups	Number of setups required
Engineering costs for product modifications	Number of modifications

Departmental Accounting

Primary goals

- Provide information for managers to use in performance evaluation.
- Assign costs to managers who are responsible for controlling the costs.

Departmental Accounting

Large complex businesses are divided into departments enabling managers to have a smaller effective span of control.

Departmental Accounting

Departments are established for specialized functions.

- **Production**
- **Sales**
- **Service**

Information for Departmental Evaluation

The accounting system provides information about resources used and outputs achieved.

Managers use this information to:

- Allocate resources.
- Control operations.
  - **Appraise performance**
  - **Corrective Action**

Information for Departmental Evaluation

The type of accounting information provided depends on whether the department is a . . .

- **Cost center** → **Evaluated on ability to control costs.**
- **Profit center** → **Evaluated on ability to generate revenues in excess of expenses.**

Information for Departmental Evaluation

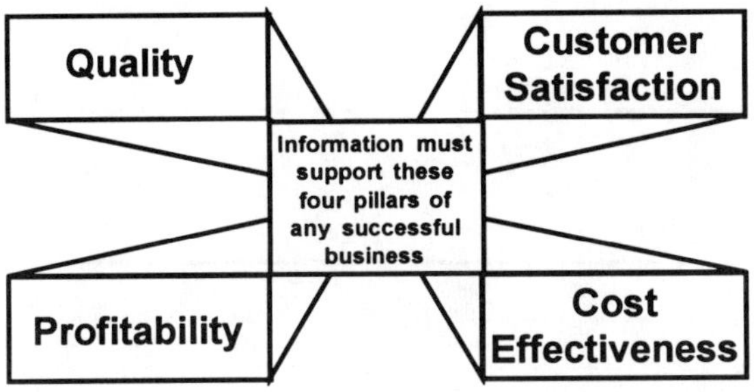

Departmental Expense Allocation

Direct expenses are incurred for the sole benefit of a specific department.

Indirect expenses benefit more than one department and are allocated among departments benefited.

Illustration of Indirect Expense Allocation

Exh. 22-9

Classic Jewelry pays its janitorial service $300 per month to clean its store. Management allocates this cost to its three departments according to the floor space each occupies.

Department	Square Feet	Percent of Total		Total Cost		Allocated Cost
Jewelry	1,000	?	×	?	=	?
Watch repair	600	?	×	?	=	?
China and silver	2,400	?	×	?	=	?
Total	4,000	100%				

Bases for Allocating Service Department Costs

Exh. 22-10

Service department costs are shared, indirect expenses that support the activities of two or more production departments.

Service Department	Common Allocation Bases
General Office	Number of employees
Personnel	Number of employees
Payroll	Number of employees
Advertising	Sales
Purchasing	Number of Purchase Orders
Cleaning	Floor space occupied
Maintenance	Floor space occupied

Service Department Costs Question

ABCO allocates its $300,000 personnel cost to operating departments based on the number of employees in each department. The assembly department has 100 employees and the packing department has 150 employees. What amount of cost is allocated to assembly?

a. $100,000
b. $120,000
c. $150,000
d. $180,000

Preparing Departmental Income Statements

Let's prepare departmental income statements using the following steps:

❶ Direct expense accumulation.
❷ Indirect expense allocation.
❸ Service department expense allocation.

Step 1: Direct Expense Accumulation

Direct expenses are traced to each department without allocation.

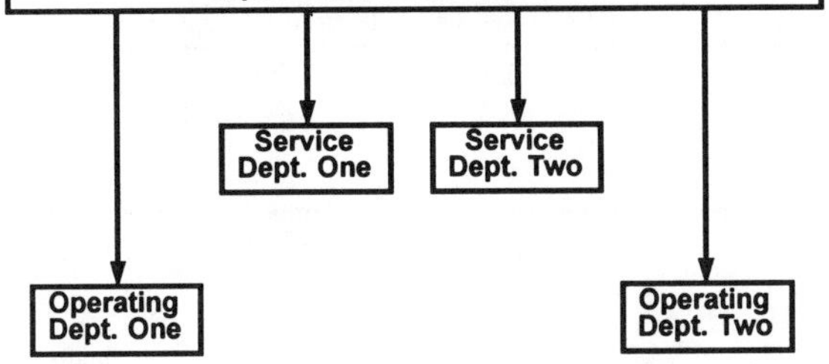

Step 2: Indirect Expense Allocation

Indirect expenses are allocated to all departments using appropriate allocation bases.

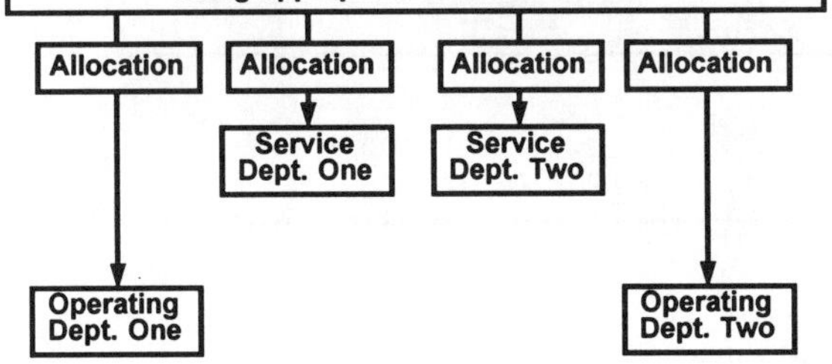

Step 3: Service Department Expense Allocation

Service department total expenses (original direct expenses + allocated indirect expenses) are allocated to operating departments.

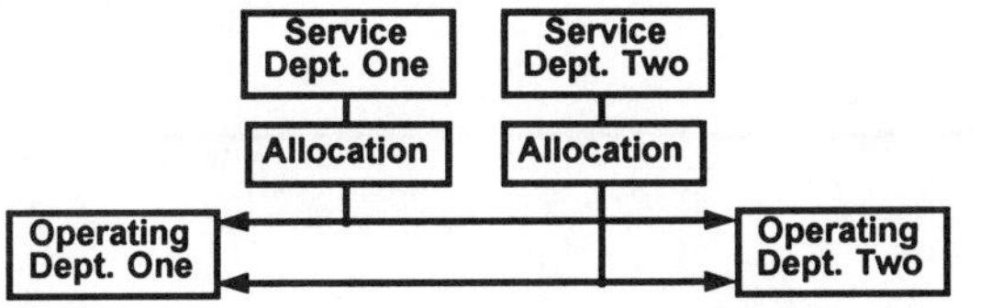

Departmental Expense Allocation Spreadsheet

	Allocation Base	Total Expense	Expense Allocation to Departments: Service Dept. One	Service Dept. Two	Sales Dept. One	Sales Dept. Two
Direct expenses						
Salaries	Payroll	$ 20,000	$ 1,000	$ 2,000	$ 6,000	$ 11,000
Supplies	Requisitions	1,500	100	300	400	700
Indirect expenses						
Rent	Floor space	10,000	1,000	1,000	3,000	5,000
Utilities	Floor space	1,000	100	100	300	500
Total dept. expenses		$ 32,500	$ 2,200	$ 3,400	$ 9,700	$ 17,200
Service dept. expenses						
Service Dept. One	Sales		(2,200)		1,000	1,200
Service Dept. Two	Employees			(3,400)	1,400	2,000
Total expenses		$ 32,500	$ 0	$ 0	$ 12,100	$ 20,400

Departmental Income Statements

	Combined	Sales Dept. One	Sales Dept. Two
Sales	$ 88,000	$ 40,000	$ 48,000
Cost of goods sold	38,000	20,000	18,000
Gross profit on sales	$ 50,000	$ 20,000	$ 30,000
Operating expenses			
Salaries	$ 17,000	$ 6,000	$ 11,000
Supplies	1,100	400	700
Rent	8,000	3,000	5,000
Utilities	800	300	500
Service Department One	2,200	1,000	1,200
Service Department Two	3,400	1,400	2,000
Total operating expenses	$ 32,500	$ 12,100	$ 20,400
Net Income	$ 17,500	$ 7,900	$ 9,600

Irwin/McGraw-Hill
© The McGraw-Hill Companies, Inc., 1999

Departmental Contribution to Overhead

Departmental revenue
– Direct expenses
= Departmental contribution

Departmental contribution . . .

- Is used to evaluate departmental performance.
- Is not a function of arbitrary allocations of indirect expenses.

A department may be eliminated when its departmental contribution is negative.

Irwin/McGraw-Hill
© The McGraw-Hill Companies, Inc., 1999

Eliminating an Unprofitable Department

As a general rule, a department can be considered a candidate for elimination if its revenues are less than its escapable expenses.

- Direct expenses are usually escapable.
- Indirect expenses are usually inescapable.

Departmental Contribution to Overhead

	Combined	Sales Dept. One	Sales Dept. Two
Sales	$ 88,000	$ 40,000	$ 48,000
Cost of goods sold	38,000	20,000	18,000
Gross profit on sales	$ 50,000	$ 20,000	$ 30,000
Direct expenses			
Salaries	$ 17,000	$ 6,000	$ 11,000
Supplies	1,100	400	700
Total direct expenses	$ 18,100	$ 6,400	$ 11,700
Departmental Contribution	$ 31,900	$ 13,600	$ 18,300
Indirect expenses			
Rent	8,000		
Utilities	800		
Service Department One	2,200		
Service Department Two	3,400		
Total indirect expenses	$ 14,400		
Net income	$ 17,500		

Controllable Costs

Costs are controllable if the manager has the power to determine, or strongly influence, the amounts incurred.

A manager's performance evaluation should be based on controllable costs.

Distinguishing Controllable and Direct Costs

Direct costs are traced to departments, but may not be controllable by the department manager.

- Example: Department managers usually have no control over their own salaries.

Controllable costs are identified with a particular manager and a definite time period.

- All costs are controllable at some level of management if the time period is long enough.

Responsibility Accounting

An accounting system that provides information . . .

- **Relating to the responsibilities of individual managers.**
- **To evaluate managers on controllable items.**

Successful implementation of responsibility accounting may use organization charts with clear lines of authority and clearly defined levels of responsibility.

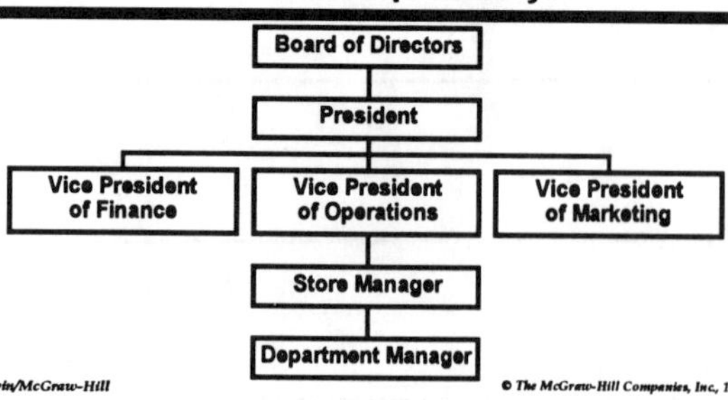

Responsibility Accounting Performance Reports

Amount of detail varies according to level in organization.

A department manager receives detailed reports.

A store manager receives summarized information from each department.

Responsibility Accounting Performance Reports

Amount of detail varies according to level in organization.

Management by exception: Upper-level management does not receive operating detail unless problems arise.

The vice president of operations receives summarized information from each store.

Responsibility Accounting Performance Reports

To be of maximum benefit, responsibility reports should . . .

- Be timely.
- Be issued regularly.
- Be understandable.
- Compare budgeted and actual amounts.

Joint Costs

A single cost incurred in producing or purchasing two or more different products.

- Similar to an indirect expense since it is shared among more than one cost object.
- Example: The cost of crude oil is a joint cost for many petrochemical products.

Allocating Joint Costs

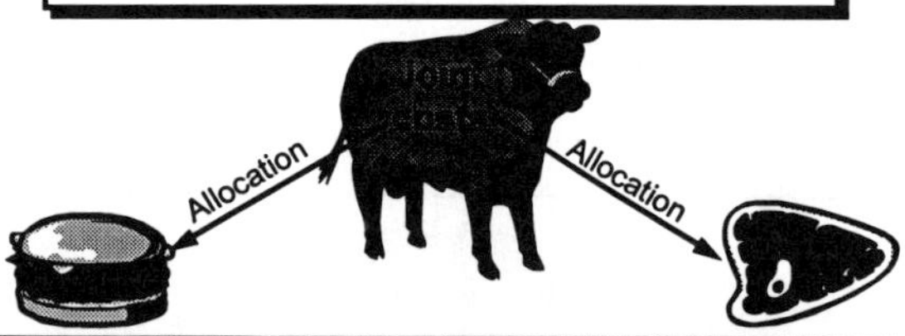

If we allocate the joint costs of raising the animal to the two products based on weight, which product would receive the largest cost allocation?

Allocating Joint Costs

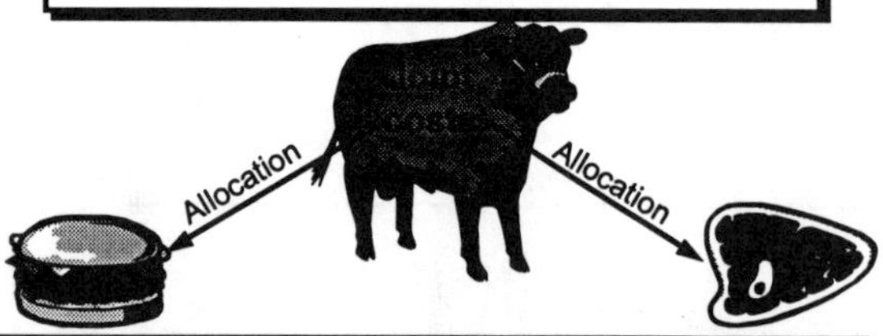

If we allocate the joint costs of raising the animal to the two products based on sales value, would the steak receive a greater portion of the cost allocation?

Allocating Joint Costs on a Value Basis

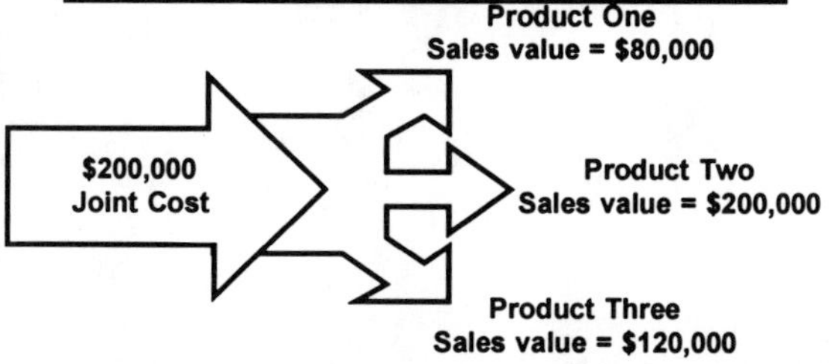

Allocate the $200,000 joint cost based on sales value.

Allocating Joint Costs on a Value Basis

Product	Value	Percent of Total		Joint Cost		Allocated Cost
One	$ 80,000	20%	×	$ 200,000	=	$ 40,000
Two	200,000	50%	×	200,000	=	100,000
Three	120,000	30%	×	200,000	=	60,000
Total	$ 400,000	100%				$ 200,000

23 CHAPTER Cost-Volume-Profit Analysis

Questions Addressed by Cost-Volume-Profit Analysis

CVP analysis is used to answer questions such as:

- How much must I sell to earn my desired income?
- How will income be affected if I reduce selling prices to increase sales volume?
- How will income be affected if I change the sales mix of my products?

Irwin/McGraw-Hill
© The McGraw-Hill Companies, Inc, 1999

Total Fixed Cost

Total fixed costs remain unchanged when activity changes.

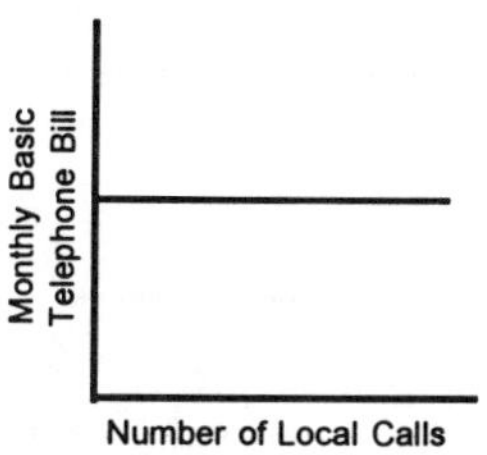

Your monthly basic telephone bill probably does not change when you make more local calls.

Irwin/McGraw-Hill
© The McGraw-Hill Companies, Inc, 1999

Fixed Cost Per Unit

Fixed costs per unit decline as activity increases.

Your average cost per local call decreases as more local calls are made.

Irwin/McGraw-Hill

Total Variable Cost

Total variable costs change when activity changes.

Your total long distance telephone bill is based on how many minutes you talk.

Irwin/McGraw-Hill

Variable Cost Per Unit

Variable costs per unit do not change as activity increases.

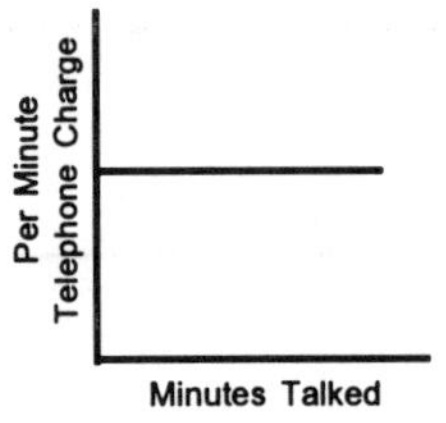

The cost per long distance minute talked is constant. For example, 10 cents per minute.

Irwin/McGraw-Hill

Cost Behavior Summary

Summary of Variable and Fixed Cost Behavior		
Cost	**In Total**	**Per Unit**
Variable	**Changes as activity level changes.**	**Remains the same over wide ranges of activity.**
Fixed	**Remains the same even when activity level changes.**	**Dereases as activity level increases.**

Mixed Costs

Mixed costs contain a fixed portion that is incurred even when facility is unused, and a variable portion that increases with usage.

Example: monthly electric utility charge

- Fixed service fee
- Variable charge per kilowatt hour used

Irwin/McGraw-Hill
© The McGraw-Hill Companies, Inc, 1999

Mixed Costs

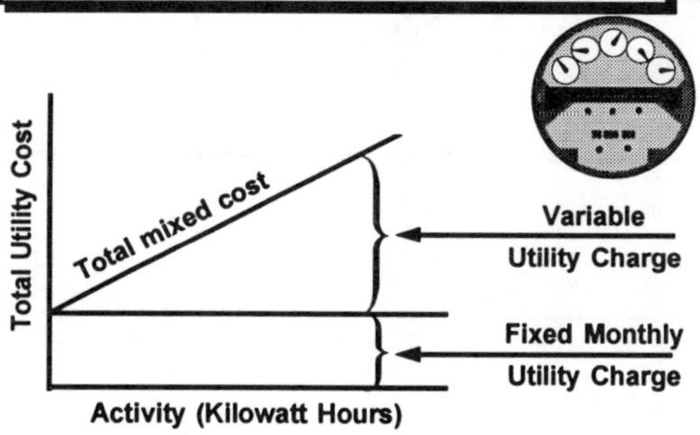

Irwin/McGraw-Hill
© The McGraw-Hill Companies, Inc, 1999

Step-Wise Costs

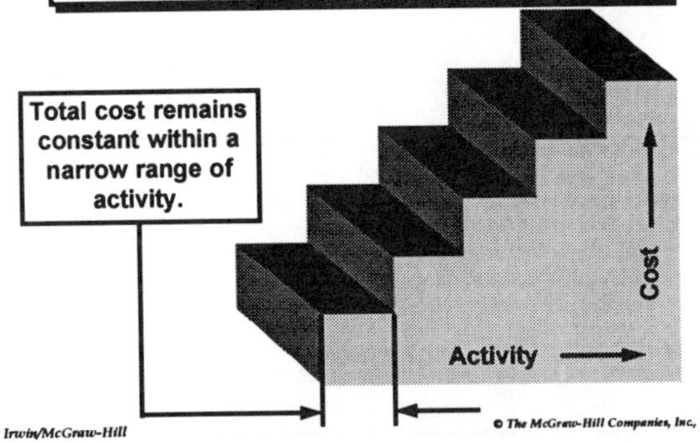

Step-Wise Costs

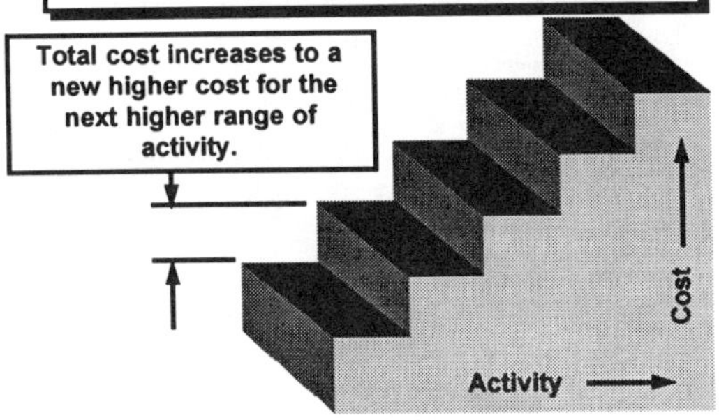

Curvilinear Costs

Costs that increase when activity increases, but in a nonlinear manner.

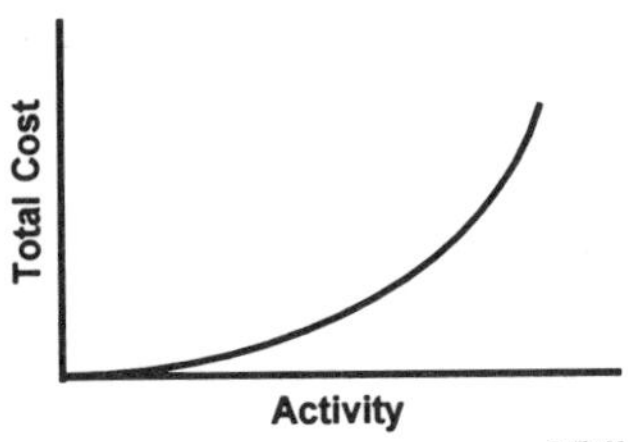

Scatter Diagram

A scatter diagram of past cost behavior may be helpful in analyzing mixed costs.

Scatter Diagram

Plot the data points on a graph (total cost vs. activity).

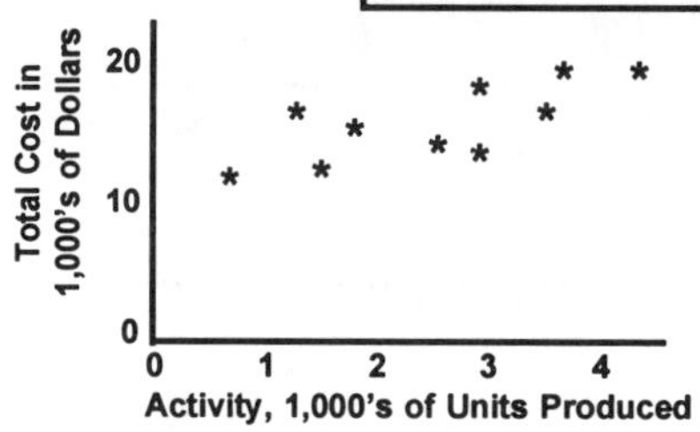

Scatter Diagram

Draw a line through the plotted data points so that about equal numbers of points fall above and below the line.

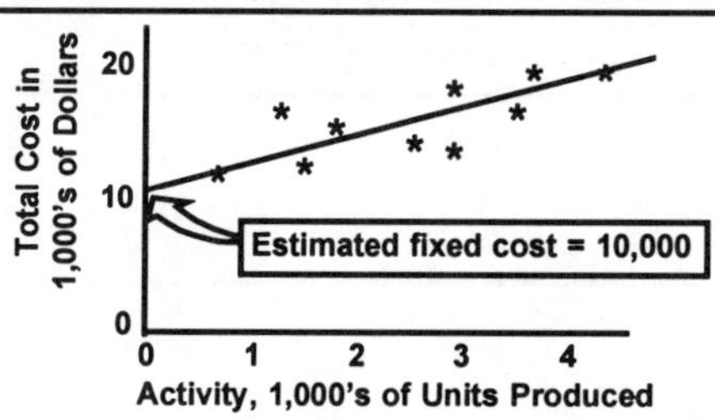

Scatter Diagram

Unit Variable Cost = Slope = $\frac{\blacktriangle \text{ in cost}}{\blacktriangle \text{ in units}}$

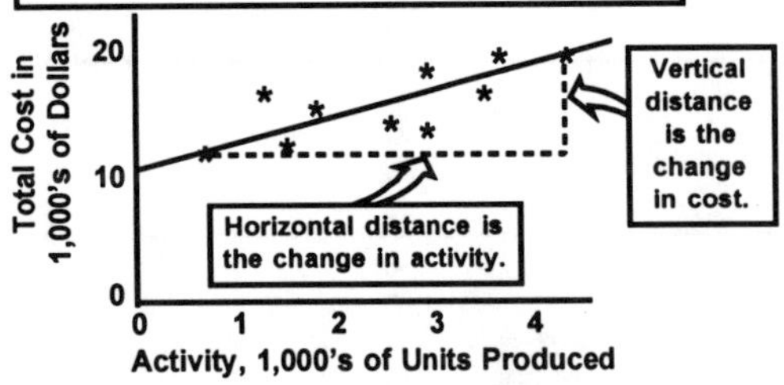

Exh. 23-6

The High-Low Method

The following relationships between sales and costs are observed:

	Sales	Cost
High activity level	$ 67,500	$ 29,000
Low activity level	17,500	20,500
Change	$ 50,000	$ 8,500

Using these two levels of activity, compute:

❶ the variable cost per unit.

❷ the total fixed cost.

Exh. 23-6

The High-Low Method

	Sales	Cost
High activity level	$ 67,500	$ 29,000
Low activity level	17,500	20,500
Change	$ 50,000	$ 8,500

❶ Unit variable cost = $\frac{\blacktriangle \text{ in cost}}{\blacktriangle \text{ in units}} = \frac{\$8,500}{\$50,000}$ = $0.17 per $

❷ Fixed cost = Total cost – Total variable cost

Fixed cost = $29,000 – ($0.17 per sales $ × $67,500)

Fixed cost = $29,000 – $11,475 = $17,525

Least-Squares Regression

Least-squares regression is usually covered in advanced cost accounting courses. It is commonly used with computer software because of the large number of calculations required.

The objective of the cost analysis remains the same: determination of total fixed cost and the variable unit cost.

Computing Break-Even Point

The break-even point (expressed in units of product or dollars of sales) is the unique sales level at which a company earns neither a profit nor incurs a loss.

Computing Break-Even Point

	Total	Unit
Sales Revenue (2,000 units)	$ 100,000	$ 50
Less: Variable costs	60,000	30
Contribution margin	$ 40,000	$ 20
Less: Fixed costs	30,000	
Net income	$ 10,000	

Contribution margin is amount by which revenue exceeds the variable costs of producing the revenue.

Computing Break-Even Point

	Total	Unit
Sales Revenue (2,000 units)	$100,000	$ 50
Less: Variable costs	60,000	30
Contribution margin	$ 40,000	$ 20
Less: Fixed costs	30,000	
Net income	$ 10,000	

How much contribution margin must this company have to cover its fixed costs (break even)?

Computing Break-Even Point

	Total	Unit
Sales Revenue (2,000 units)	$100,000	$ 50
Less: Variable costs	60,000	30
Contribution margin	$ 40,000	$ 20
Less: Fixed costs	30,000	
Net income	$ 10,000	

How many units must this company sell to cover its fixed costs (break even)?

Formula for Computing Break-Even Sales (in Units)

Exh. 23-8

We have just seen one of the basic CVP relationships – the break-even computation.

$$\text{Break-even point in units} = \frac{\text{Fixed costs}}{\text{Contribution margin per unit}}$$

Unit sales price less unit variable cost ($20 in previous example)

Formula for Computing Break-Even Sales (in Dollars)

Exh. 23-9

The break-even formula may also be expressed in sales dollars.

$$\text{Break-even point in dollars} = \frac{\text{Fixed costs}}{\text{Contribution margin ratio}}$$

$$\frac{\text{Unit sales price}}{\text{Unit variable cost}}$$

Computing Break-Even Sales Question 1

ABC Co. sells product XYZ at $5.00 per unit. If fixed costs are $200,000 and variable costs are $3.00 per unit, how many units must be sold to break even?

a. 100,000 units
b. 40,000 units
c. 200,000 units
d. 66,667 units

Computing Break-Even Sales Question 2

Use the contribution margin ratio formula to determine the amount of sales revenue ABC must have to break even. All information remains unchanged: fixed costs are $200,000; unit sales price is $5.00; and unit variable cost is $3.00.

a. $200,000
b. $300,000
c. $400,000
d. $500,000

Preparing a CVP Chart

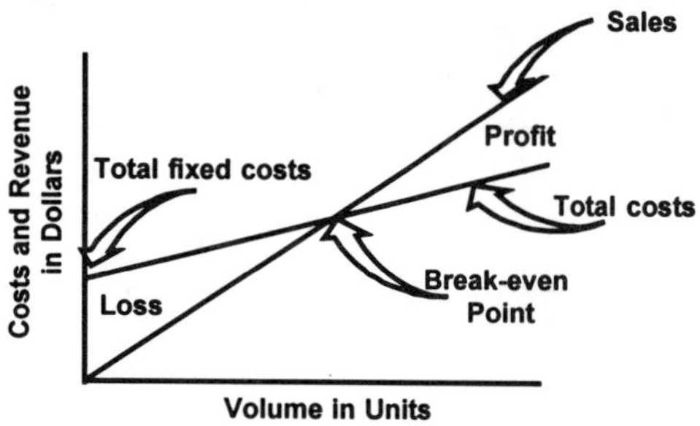

Assumptions of CVP Analysis

❶ A limited range of activity called the relevant range, where CVP relationships are linear.
- ✓ Unit selling price remains constant.
- ✓ Unit variable costs remain constant.
- ✓ Total fixed cost remain constant.

❷ Production = sales (no inventory changes).

Computing Income from Expected Sales

Exh. 23-12

Income = Sales - [Fixed costs + Variable costs]

or

Income = Sales - Fixed costs - Variable costs

Exh. 23-13

Computing Income from Expected Sales

Rydell expects to sell 1,500 units at $100 each next month. Fixed costs are $24,000 per month and the unit variable cost is $70. What amount of income should Rydell expect?

Income = Sales - Fixed costs - Variable costs

Income = [1,500 units × $100] - $24,000 - [1,500 units × $70]

Income = $21,000

Computing Income from Expected Sales

Break-even formulas may be adjusted to show the sales volume needed to earn any amount of income.

$$\text{Unit sales} = \frac{\text{Fixed costs + Target income}}{\text{Contribution margin per unit}}$$

$$\text{Dollar sales} = \frac{\text{Fixed costs + Target income}}{\text{Contribution margin ratio}}$$

Computing Income from Expected Sales - Question

ABC Co. sells product XYZ at $5.00 per unit. If fixed costs are $200,000 and variable costs are $3.00 per unit, how many units must be sold to earn income of $40,000?

a. 100,000 units
b. 120,000 units
c. 80,000 units
d. 200,000 units

Formula for Computing Sales (Dollars) for a Target Net Income

Exh. 23-14

Target net income is income after income tax.

$$\text{Dollar sales} = \frac{\text{Fixed costs} + \text{Target net income} + \text{Income taxes}}{\text{Contribution margin ratio}}$$

Computing Sales (Dollars) for a Target Net Income

To convert target net income to before-tax income, use the following formula:

$$\text{Before-tax income} = \frac{\text{Target net income}}{1 - \text{tax rate}}$$

Computing Sales (Dollars) for a Target Net Income

Rydell has a monthly target net income of $18,000. The unit selling price is $100. Monthly fixed costs are $24,000, the unit variable cost is $70, and the tax rate is 25 percent.

What is Rydell's before-tax income and income tax expense?

Computing Sales (Dollars) for a Target Net Income

Rydell has a monthly target net income of $18,000. The unit selling price is $100. Monthly fixed costs are $24,000, the unit variable cost is $70, and the tax rate is 25 percent.

What monthly sales revenue will Rydell need to earn the target net income?

Exh. 23-17

Computing the Margin of Safety

Margin of safety is the amount by which sales may decline before reaching break-even sales.

Margin of safety may be expressed as a percentage of expected sales.

$$\text{Margin of safety percentage} = \frac{\text{Expected sales - Break-even sales}}{\text{Expected sales}}$$

Exh. 23-17

Computing the Margin of Safety

If Rydell's sales are $100,000 and break-even sales are $80,000, what is the margin of safety in dollars and as a percentage?

$$\text{Margin of safety percentage} = \frac{\text{Expected sales - Break-even sales}}{\text{Expected sales}}$$

Sensitivity Analysis

The basic CVP relationships may be used to analyze a number of situations such as changing sales price, changing variable cost, or changing fixed cost.

Consider the following example.

Continue

Sensitivity Analysis Example

Rydell Company is considering buying a new machine that would increase monthly fixed costs from $24,000 to $30,000, but decrease unit variable costs from $70 to $60. The $100 per unit selling price would remain unchanged.

What is the new break-even point in dollars?

Computing Multiproduct Break-Even Point

The CVP formulas may be modified for use when a company sells more than one product.

- The unit contribution margin is replaced with the contribution margin for a composite unit.
- A composite unit is composed of specific numbers of each product in proportion to the product sales mix.
- Sales mix is the ratio of the volumes of the various products.

Computing Multiproduct Break-Even Point

The resulting break-even formula for composite unit sales is:

$$\text{Break-even point in composite units} = \frac{\text{Fixed costs}}{\text{Contribution margin per composite unit}}$$

Consider the following example:

Continue

Computing Multiproduct Break-Even Point

Hair-Today offers three cuts as shown below. Annual fixed costs are $96,000. Compute the break-even point in composite units and in number of units for each haircut at the given sales mix.

	Haircuts		
	Basic	Ultra	Budget
Selling Price	$ 10.00	$ 16.00	$ 8.00
Variable Cost	6.50	9.00	4.00
Unit Contribution	$ 3.50	$ 7.00	$ 4.00
Sales Mix Ratio	4	2	1

Computing Multiproduct Break-Even Point

Step 1: Compute contribution margin per composite unit.

	Haircuts			
	Basic	Ultra	Budget	
Selling Price	$10.00	$16.00	$8.00	
Variable Cost	6.50	9.00	4.00	
Unit Contribution	$3.50	$7.00	$4.00	
Sales Mix Ratio	× 4	× 2	× 1	
Weighted Contribution	$14.00 +	$14.00 +	$ 4.00 =	$ 32.00

Contribution margin per composite unit

Computing Multiproduct Break-Even Point

Exh. 23-19

Step 2: Compute break-even point in composite units.

Break-even point in composite units = Fixed costs / Contribution margin per composite unit

Break-even point in composite units = \$96,000 / \$32.00 per composite unit

Break-even point in composite units = 3,000 composite units

Computing Multiproduct Break-Even Point

Step 3: Determine the number of each haircut that must be sold to break even.

Product	Sales Mix		Composite Cuts		Haircuts
Basic	4	×	3,000	=	12,000
Ultra	2	×	3,000	=	6,000
Budget	1	×	3,000	=	3,000

Multiproduct Break-Even Income Statement

Exh. 23-20

Step 4: Verify the results.

	Haircuts Basic	Haircuts Ultra	Haircuts Budget	Combined
Selling Price	\$ 10.00	\$ 16.00	\$ 8.00	
Variable Cost	6.50	9.00	4.00	
Unit Contribution	\$ 3.50	\$ 7.00	\$ 4.00	
Sales Volume	× 12,000	× 6,000	× 3,000	
Total Contribution	\$ 42,000	\$ 42,000	\$ 12,000	\$ 96,000
Fixed Costs				96,000
Income				\$ 0

Operating Leverage

A measure of the extent to which fixed costs are being used in an organization.

A measure of how a percentage change in sales will affect profits.

$$\frac{\text{Contribution margin}}{\text{Net income}} = \text{Degree of operating leverage}$$

Operating Leverage

Rydell Company

Sales (1,600 units)	$160,000
Less: variable expenses	112,000
Contribution margin	48,000
Less: fixed expenses	24,000
Net income	$ 24,000

$$\frac{\text{Contribution margin}}{\text{Net income}} = \text{Degree of operating leverage}$$

$$\frac{\$48,000}{\$24,000} = 2.0$$

If Rydell increases sales by 10 percent, what will the percentage increase in income be?

Operating Leverage

Rydell Company

Sales (1,600 units)	$160,000
Less: variable expenses	112,000
Contribution margin	48,000
Less: fixed expenses	24,000
Net income	$ 24,000

Percent increase in sales	10%
Degree of operating leverage	× 2
Percent increase in income	20%

24 CHAPTER Master Budgets and Planning

Importance of Budgeting

Advantages

- Defines goals and objectives
- Promotes analysis and a focus on the future
- Motivates Employees
- Provides a basis for evaluating performance
- Coordinates business activities
- Communicates plans and instructions

Budget Committee

Consists of managers from all departments of the organization.

Provides central guidance to insure that individual budgets submitted from all departments are realistic and coordinated.

Budget Committee

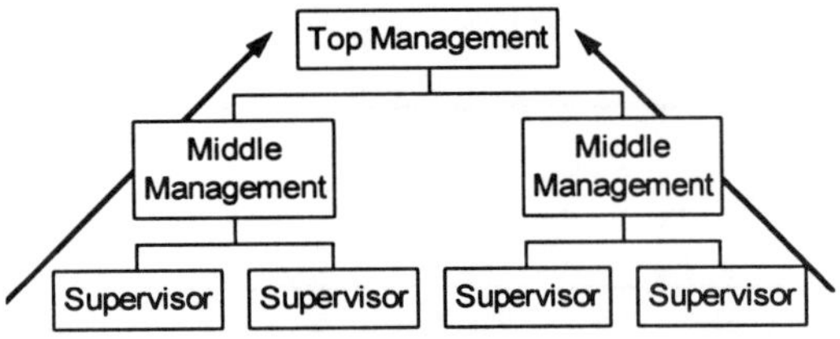

Flow of Budget Data is a bottom-up process.

Budget Period

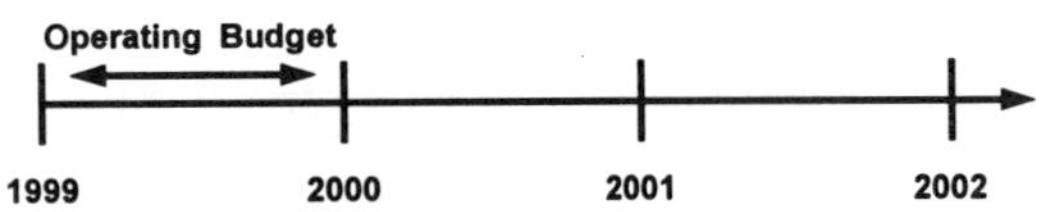

The annual operating budget may be divided into quarterly or monthly budgets.

Budget Period

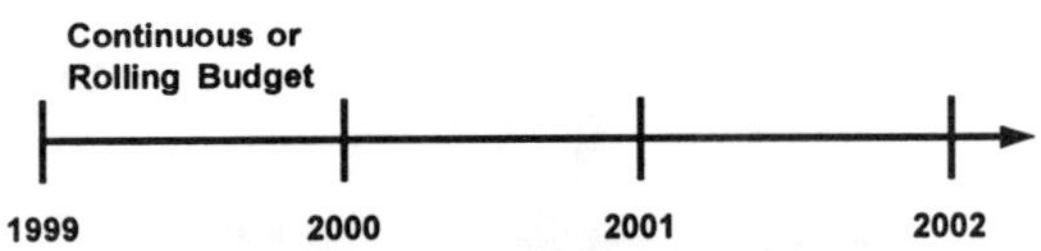

The budget may be a twelve-month budget that rolls forward one month as the current month is completed.

Master Budget Sequence

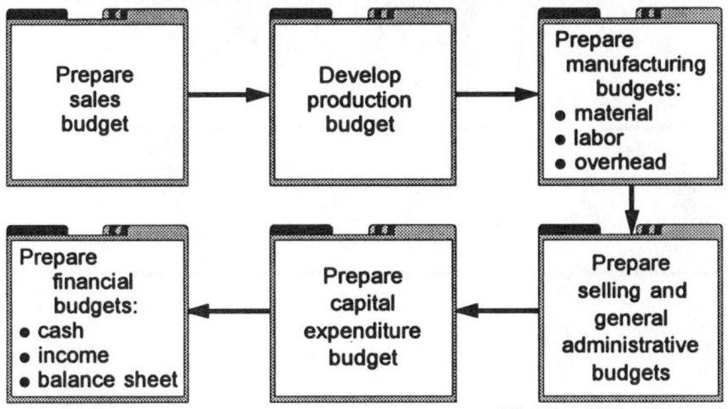

Preparing the Sales Budget

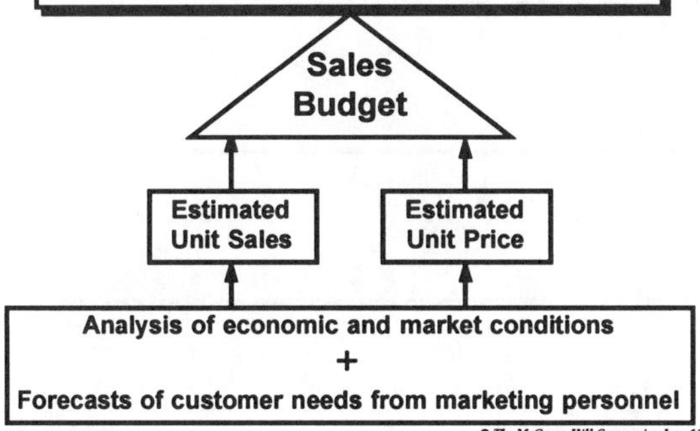

Preparing the Sales Budget

In September 1999, Hockey Den sold 7,000 hockey pucks at $10 each. Hockey Den prepared the following sales budget for the next four months:

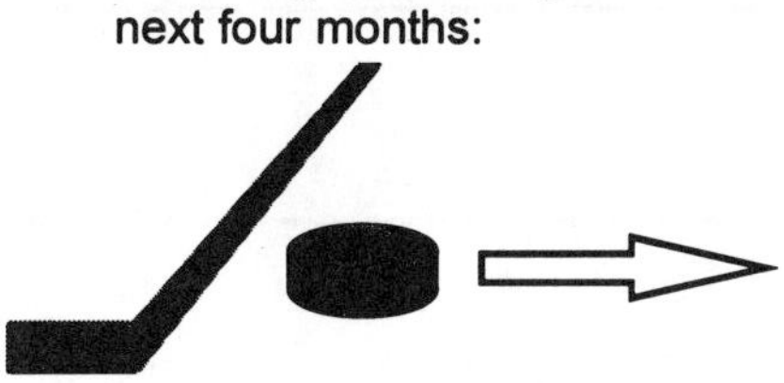

Preparing the Sales Budget

Exh. 24-6

HOCKEY DEN
Monthly Sales Budget
October 1999 – January 2000

	Budgeted Unit Sales	Budgeted Unit Price	Budgeted Total Sales
September 1999 (actual)	7,000	$ 10	$ 70,000
October 1999	10,000	$ 10	$ 100,000
November 1999	8,000	10	80,000
December 1999	14,000	10	140,000
Total	32,000	$ 10	$ 320,000
January 2000	9,000	$ 10	$ 90,000

Preparing the Merchandise Purchases Budget

The quantity purchased is affected by:

Just-in-time inventory systems that enable purchases of smaller, frequently delivered quantities.

Safety stock inventory systems that provide protection against lost sales caused by delays in supplier shipments.

Preparing the Merchandise Purchases Budget

Exh. 24-8

Inventory to be purchased = Budgeted ending inventory + Budgeted sales for the period − Budgeted beginning inventory

Hockey Den buys hockey pucks for $6.00 each and maintains an ending inventory equal to 90 percent of the next month's budgeted sales. 9,000 hockey pucks are on hand on September 30.

Let's prepare the purchases budget for Hockey Den.

Preparing the Merchandise Purchases Budget

Exh. 24-9

HOCKEY DEN
Merchandise Purchases Budget
October 1999 – December 1999

	October	November	December
Next month's unit sales	8,000	14,000	9,000
Ending inventory percentage	× 90%	× 90%	× 90%
Budgeted ending inventory units	7,200	12,600	8,100
Add current month's unit sales	10,000	8,000	14,000
Total units needed	17,200	20,600	22,100
Deduct beginning inventory units	9,000	7,200	12,600
Number of units to be purchased	8,200	13,400	9,500
Budgeted cost per unit	× $ 6	× $ 6	× $ 6
Budgeted cost of purchases	$ 49,200	$ 80,400	$ 57,000

Beginning inventory is last month's ending inventory.

Irwin/McGraw-Hill

Preparing the Selling Expense Budget

- Hockey Den pays sales commissions equal to 10 percent of total sales.
- Hockey Den pays a monthly salary of $2,000 to its sales manager.

Let's prepare the sales budget for Hockey Den.

Irwin/McGraw-Hill

Selling Expense Budget

Exh. 24-14

HOCKEY DEN
Selling Expense Budget
October 1999 – December 1999

	October	November	December	Total
Budgeted sales	$ 100,000	$ 80,000	$ 140,000	$ 320,000
Sales commission %	× 10%	× 10%	× 10%	× 10%
Sales commission	$ 10,000	$ 8,000	$ 14,000	$ 32,000
Sales manager salary	2,000	2,000	2,000	6,000
Total selling expenses	$ 12,000	$ 10,000	$ 16,000	$ 38,000

Irwin/McGraw-Hill

Preparing the General and Administrative Expense Budget

- General and administrative salaries are $4,500 per month.
- Depreciation of equipment is $1,500 per month.

Let's prepare the general and administrative expense budget for Hockey Den.

General and Administrative Expense Budget

Exh. 24-15

HOCKEY DEN
General and Administrative Expense budget
October 1999 – December 1999

	October	November	December	Total
Administrative salaries	$ 4,500	$ 4,500	$ 4,500	$ 13,500
Equipment depreciation	1,500	1,500	1,500	4,500
Total	$ 6,000	$ 6,000	$ 6,000	$ 18,000

Preparing Financial Budgets

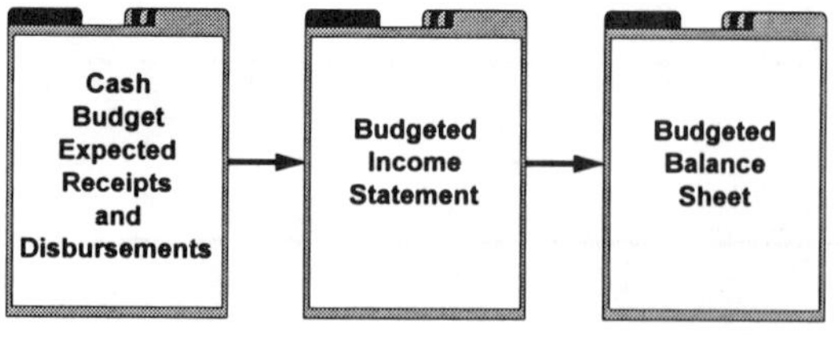

Budgeted Cash Receipts

- Forty percent of Hockey Den's sales are for cash.
- The remaining sixty percent are credit sales that are collected in full in the month following sale.

Let's prepare the cash receipts budget for Hockey Den.

Cash Receipts Budgeted

Exh. 24-17

HOCKEY DEN
Cash Receipts Budget
October 1999 – December 1999

	September	October	November	December
Budgeted sales	$ 70,000	$ 100,000	$ 80,000	$ 140,000
Accounts receivable	$ 42,000	$ 60,000	$ 48,000	$ 84,000
Cash receipts from:				
Cash sales		$ 40,000	$ 32,000	$ 56,000
Collection of receivables		42,000	60,000	48,000
Total cash receipts		$ 82,000	$ 92,000	$ 104,000

Cash Disbursements for Purchases

- Hockey Den's purchases of merchandise are entirely on account.
- Full payment is made in the month following purchase.
- The September 30 balance of Accounts Payable is $58,200.

Let's look at cash disbursements for purchases for Hockey Den.

Cash Disbursements for Purchases

Exh. 24-18

HOCKEY DEN Cash Disbursements for Purchases October - December 1999	
October payments (September 30 balance)	$ 58,200
November payments (October purchases)	49,200
December payments (November purchases)	80,400

Preparing the Cash Budget

Hockey Den:

- Will pay a cash dividend of $3,000 in November.
- Will purchase $25,000 of equipment in December.
- Has an income tax liability of $20,000 from the previous quarter that will be paid in October.
- Has a September 30 cash balance of $20,000.
- Has an agreement with its bank for loans at the end of each month to enable a minimum cash balance of $20,000.

Continue

Preparing the Cash Budget

Hockey Den:

- Pays interest equal to one percent of the prior month's ending loan balance.
- Repays loans when the ending cash balance exceeds $20,000.
- Owes $10,000 on this loan arrangement on September 30.
- Has 40 percent income tax rate.
- Will pay taxes for current quarter next year.

Let's prepare the cash budget for Hockey Den.

Exh. 24-16

HOCKEY DEN
Cash Budget
October 1999 - December 1999

	October	November	December
Beginning cash balance	$ 20,000	$ 20,000	$ 22,272
Receipts from customers	82,000	92,000	104,000
Total cash available	$ 102,000	$ 112,000	$ 126,272
Disbursements			
Payments for merchandise	$ 58,200	$ 49,200	$ 80,400
Sales commissions	10,000	8,000	14,000
Sales salaries	2,000	2,000	2,000
Administrative salaries	4,500	4,500	4,500
Income taxes	20,000		
Dividends		3,000	
Interest	100	228	
Equipment purchase			25,000
Total disbursements	$ 94,800	$ 66,928	$ 125,900
Preliminary balance	$ 7,200	$ 45,072	$ 372

Exh. 24-16

Cash Budget Continued

HOCKEY DEN
Cash Budget
October 1999 - December 1999

	October	November	December
Preliminary balance	$ 7,200	$ 45,072	$ 372
Additional borrowing	12,800		19,628
Loan repayment		(22,800)	
Ending cash balance	$ 20,000	$ 22,272	$ 20,000
Ending loan balance	$ 22,800	$ 0	$ 19,628

Preparing a Budgeted Income Statement

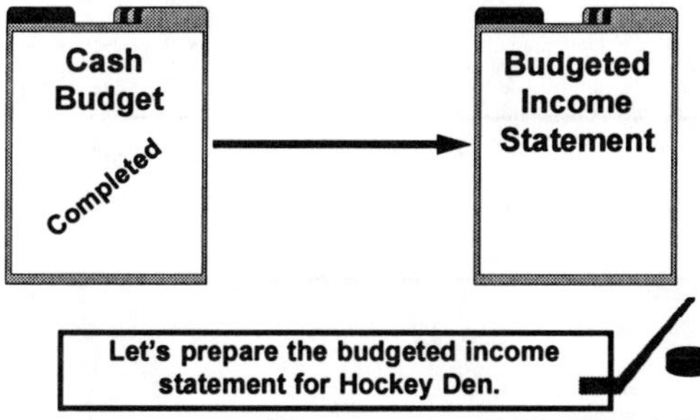

Let's prepare the budgeted income statement for Hockey Den.

Exh. 24-19

HOCKEY DEN
Budgeted Income Statement
For Three Months Ended December 31, 1999

Sales (32,000 units @ $10)		$ 320,000
Cost of goods sold (32,000 units @ $6)		192,000
Gross profit		$ 128,000
Operating expenses:		
Sales commissions	$ 32,000	
Sales salaries	6,000	
Administrative salaries	13,500	
Equipment depreciation	4,500	
Interest expense	328	56,328
Net income before taxes		$ 71,672
Income tax expense		28,669
Net income		$ 43,003

Irwin/McGraw-Hill

Preparing a Budgeted Balance Sheet

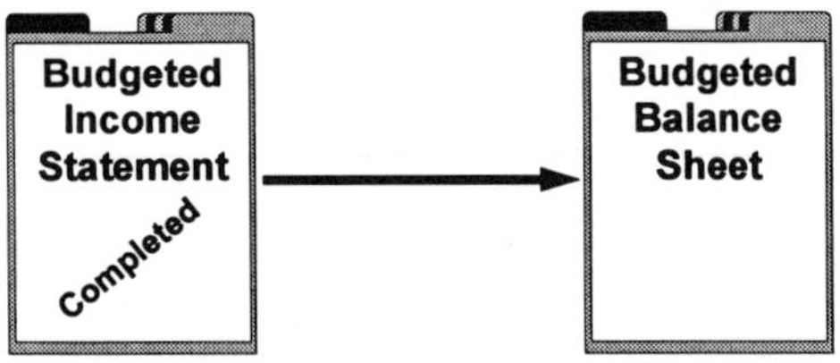

Let's prepare the budgeted balance sheet for Hockey Den.

Irwin/McGraw-Hill

Preparing a Budgeted Balance Sheet

Hockey Den reports the following account balances on September 30 prior to preparing its budgeted financial statements:

- Equipment $200,000
- Accumulated depreciation $ 36,000
- Common stock $150,000
- Retained earnings $ 41,800

Let's prepare the budgeted balance sheet for Hockey Den.

Irwin/McGraw-Hill

Exh. 24-21

HOCKEY DEN
Budgeted Balance Sheet
December 31, 1999

Assets		
Cash		$ 20,000
Accounts receivable		84,000
Inventory		48,600
Equipment	$225,000	
Less accumulated depreciation	40,500	184,500
Total assets		$337,100
Liabilities and Stockholders' Equity		
Liabilities		
Accounts payable	$ 57,000	
Income taxes payable	28,669	
Bank loan payable	19,628	$105,297
Stockholders' equity		
Common Stock	$150,000	
Retained Earnings	81,803	231,803
Total liabilities and stockholders' equity		$337,100

Manufacturing Budgets

Hockey Den is a merchandiser.

Let's now take a look at budgets unique to a manufacturer.

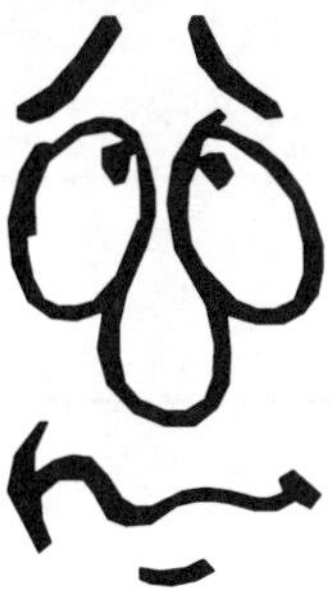

Preparing Production and Manufacturing Budgets

- Hockey Den buys hockey pucks from Hockey Supply, a manufacturer of hockey equipment.
- We will examine production and manufacturing budgets for Hockey Supply.
- Hockey Supply produces hockey pucks for Hockey Den on a special order basis in the exact quantity needed by Hockey Den to meet its sales budget.

Let's prepare the production budget for Hockey Supply.

Production Budget

HOCKEY SUPPLY
Production Budget
October 1999 – December 1999

	October	November	December
Next month's unit sales	8,000	14,000	9,000
Ending inventory percentage	× 90%	× 90%	× 90%
Budgeted ending inventory units	7,200	12,600	8,100
Add current month's unit sales	10,000	8,000	14,000
Total units needed	17,200	20,600	22,100
Deduct beginning inventory units	9,000	7,200	12,600
Number of units to be produced	8,200	13,400	9,500

Beginning inventory is last month's ending inventory.

Preparing Production and Manufacturing Budgets

A manufacturing budget shows the budgeted costs for raw materials, direct labor, and manufacturing overhead.

Irwin/McGraw-Hill
© The McGraw-Hill Companies, Inc, 1999

Direct Materials Budget

- Hockey Supply uses one-half pound of vulcanized rubber to make each puck.
- Management wants 50 percent of the next month's budgeted needs for vulcanized rubber on hand at the end of each month.
- At the end of September, 2,050 pounds of vulcanized rubber are on hand. Hockey Supply pays $2.00 per pound for vulcanized rubber.

Let's prepare the direct materials budget for Hockey Supply.

Irwin/McGraw-Hill
© The McGraw-Hill Companies, Inc, 1999

Direct Materials Budget

HOCKEY SUPPLY Direct Materials Budget October 1999 – December 1999	October	November	December
Budgeted Production (units)	8,200	13,400	9,500
Material per unit (lbs.)	× 0.5	× 0.5	× 0.5
Material needed for production (lbs.)	4,100	6,700	4,750
Add desired ending inventory (lbs.)	3,350	2,375	2,250
Total material requirements	7,450	9,075	7,000
Deduct beginning inventory units	2,050	3,350	2,375
Number of units to be purchased	5,400	5,725	4,625
Material price per pound	× $2	× $2	× $2
Total cost of Material purchases	10,800	11,450	9,250

Irwin/McGraw-Hill

Direct Labor Budget

- 15 minutes of labor time is required to produce each puck.
- The labor rate is $8.00 per hour.

Let's prepare the direct labor budget for Hockey Supply.

Irwin/McGraw-Hill

Direct Labor Budget

HOCKEY SUPPLY Direct Labor Budget October 1999 – December 1999	October	November	December
Budgeted Production (units)	8,200	13,400	9,500
Labor hours per unit	× 0.25	× 0.25	× 0.25
Total labor hours needed	2,050	3,350	2,375
Laber rate per hour	× $8	× $8	× $8
Labor Dollars	$ 16,400	$ 26,800	$ 19,000

Irwin/McGraw-Hill

Manufacturing Overhead Budget

- **Variable manufacturing overhead is $1.00 per unit produced.**
- **Fixed overhead associated with Hockey Den's business is $1,000 per month.**

Let's prepare the manufacturing overhead budget for Hockey Supply.

Manufacturing Overhead Budget

HOCKEY SUPPLY
Manufacturing Overhead Budget
October 1999 – December 1999

	October	November	December
Budgeted Production (units)	8,200	13,400	9,500
Variable overhead rate	× $ 1.00	× $ 1.00	× $ 1.00
Budgeted variable overhead	$ 8,200	$ 13,400	$ 9,500
Budgeted fixed overhead	1,000	1,000	1,000
Budgeted total overhead	$ 9,200	$ 14,400	$ 10,500

25 CHAPTER Flexible Budgets and Standard Costs

Budgetary Control and Reporting

❶ Develop the budget from planned objectives.

❷ Compare actual with budget and analyze any differences.

❸ Take corrective and strategic actions.

❹ Revise objectives and prepare a new budget.

Management uses budgets to monitor and control operations.

Fixed Budget Performance Report

Fixed budgets are prepared for a single, predicted level of activity.

Performance evaluation is difficult when actual activity differs from the predicted level of activity.

Fixed Budget Performance Report

Consider the following condensed example from the Optel Company . . .

Fixed Budget Performance Report

Exh. 25-2

Optel
Fixed Budget Performance Report
For the Month Ended November 30, 1999

	Fixed Budget	Actual Results	Variances	
Sales: In units	10,000	12,000		
In dollars	$100,000	$125,000	$ 25,000	F
Cost of goods sold	$ 49,000	$ 58,100	$ 9,100	U
Selling expenses	13,000	15,100	2,100	U
Gen. & admin. expenses	26,000	26,400	400	U
Total expenses	$ 88,000	$ 99,600	$ 11,600	U
Income from operations	$ 12,000	$ 25,400	$ 13,400	F

Fixed Budget Performance Report

Flexible Budgets

Central Concept

If you can tell me what your activity was for the period, I will tell you what your costs and revenue should have been.

Purpose of Flexible Budgets

- Show revenues and expenses that should have occurred at the actual level of activity.
- May be prepared for any activity level in the relevant range.
- Reveal variances due to good cost control or lack of cost control.
- Improve performance evaluation.

Preparing Flexible Budgets

To **flex** a budget for different activity levels, we must know how costs behave with changes in activity levels.

- Total variable costs change in direct proportion to changes in activity.
- Total fixed costs remain unchanged within the relevant range.

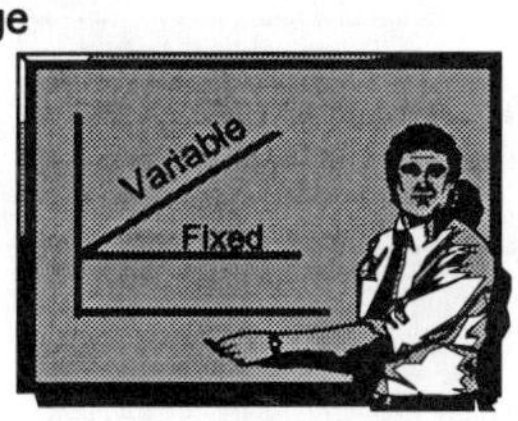

Preparing Flexible Budgets

Exh. 25-3

Optel
Flexible Budgets
For the Month Ended November 30, 1999

	Variable Amount per Unit	Total Fixed Cost	Budget for 10,000 Units	Budget for 12,000 Units	Budget for 14,000 Units
Sales:	$ 10.00		$100,000	$120,000	$140,000
Total variable costs	4.80		48,000	57,600	67,200
Contribution margin	$ 5.20		$ 52,000	$ 62,400	$ 72,800
Total fixed costs		$40,000	40,000	40,000	40,000
Income from operations			$ 12,000	$ 22,400	$ 32,800

Irwin/McGraw-Hill

Flexible Budget Performance Report

Exh. 25-4

Optel
Flexible Budget Performance Report
For the Month Ended November 30, 1999

	Variable Amount per Unit	Total Fixed Cost	Budget for 12,000 Units	Actual for 12,000 Units	Variances
Sales (12,000 units)	$ 10.00		$120,000	$125,000	$ 5,000 F
Total variable costs	4.80		57,600	59,400	1,800 U
Contribution margin	$ 5.20		$ 62,400	$ 65,600	$ 3,200 F
Total fixed costs		$40,000	40,000	40,200	200 U
Income from operations			$ 22,400	$ 25,400	$ 3,000 F

Irwin/McGraw-Hill

Standard Costs

- Based on carefully predetermined amounts.
- Used for planning labor, material and overhead requirements.
- The expected level of performance.
- Benchmarks for measuring performance.

Irwin/McGraw-Hill

Setting Standard Costs

Setting Standard Costs

Setting Standard Costs

Setting Direct Material Standards

Price Standards

Use competitive bids for the quality and quantity desired.

Quantity Standards

Use product design specifications.

Setting Direct Material Standards

The standard material cost for one unit of product is:

standard price for one unit of material × **standard quantity of material required for one unit of product**

Setting Direct Labor Standards

Rate Standards

Use wage surveys and labor contracts.

Time Standards

Use time and motion studies for each labor operation.

Setting Direct Labor Standards

The standard labor cost for one unit of product is:

standard wage rate for one hour × standard number of labor hours for one unit of product

Setting Variable Overhead Standards

Rate Standards

The rate is the variable portion of the predetermined overhead rate.

Activity Standards

The activity is the cost driver used to calculate the predetermined overhead.

Setting Variable Overhead Standards

The standard variable overhead cost for one unit of product is:

standard variable overhead rate for one unit of activity × standard number of activity units for one unit of product

Standard Cost Card

Exh. 25-5

A standard cost card might look like this:

Cost factor	Standard Quantity or Hours	Standard Price or Rate	Standard Cost
Direct materials	1 kg.	$ 25 per kg.	$ 25.00
Direct labor	2 hours	$ 20 per hour	40.00
Variable mfg. overhead	2 hours	$ 10 per hour	20.00
Total standard unit cost			$ 85.00

Variances

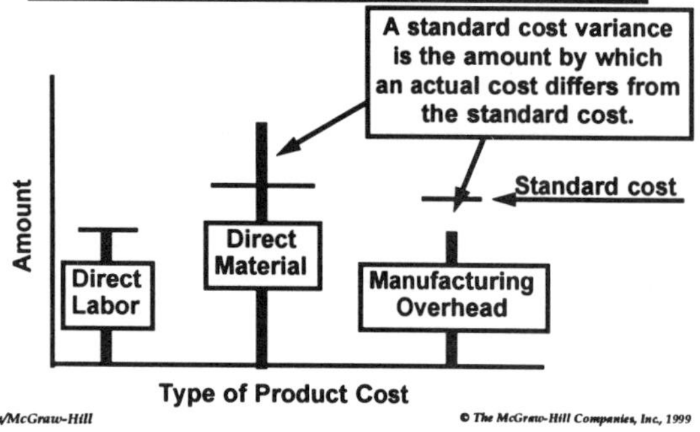

Variances

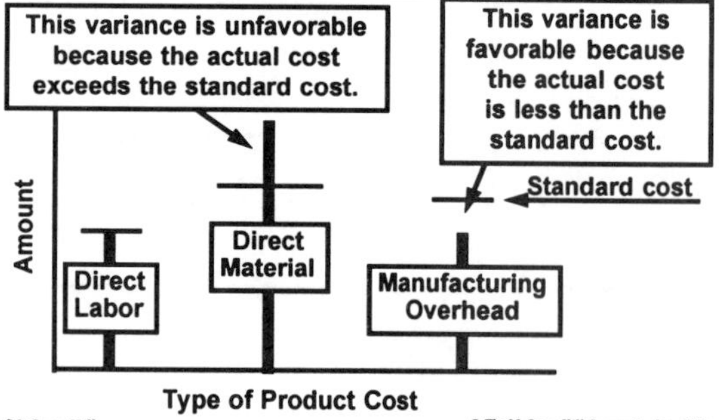

Variance Analysis

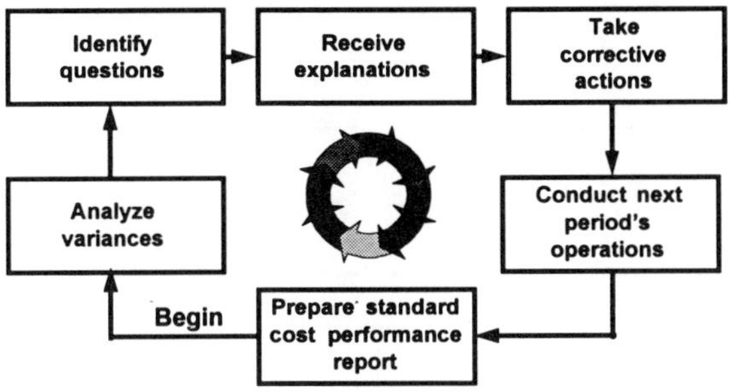

Computing Variances

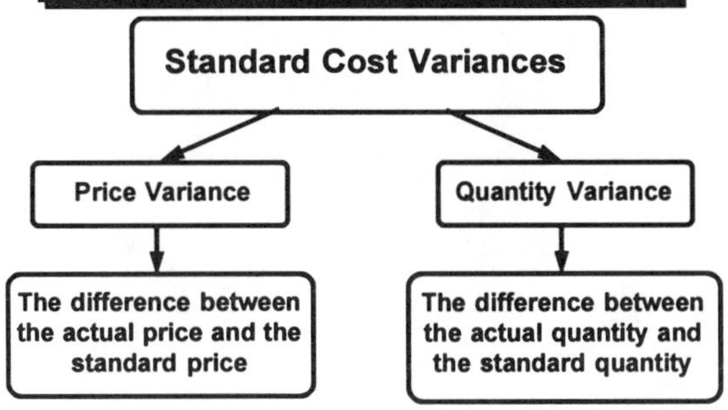

Computing Variances

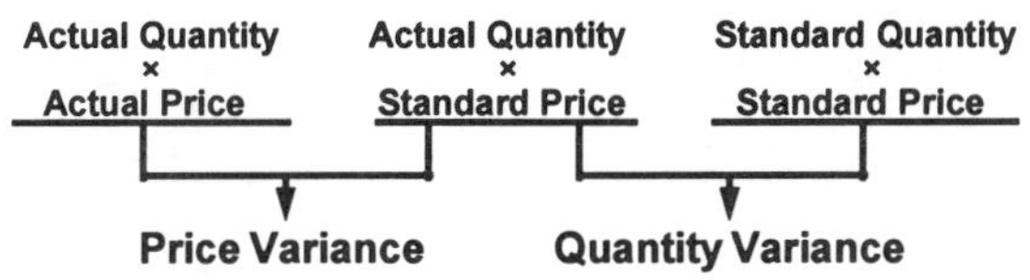

AQ(AP - SP)	SP(AQ - SQ)
AQ = Actual Quantity	SP = Standard Price
AP = Actual Price	SQ = Standard Quantity

Computing Material and Labor Variances

G-Max Company makes golf hats with the following standard cost information:

Direct materials (1 yd. per unit at $1 per yd.)	$ 1.00
Direct labor (1 hr. per unit at $6 per hr.)	6.00
Total standard direct cost per unit	$ 7.00

Material Variances

During May, G-Max produced 3,500 hats using 3,600 yards of material. G-Max paid $1.05 per yard for the material.
Compute the material price and quantity variances.

Direct materials (1 yd. per unit at $1 per yd.)	$ 1.00
Direct labor (1 hr. per unit at $6 per hr.)	6.00
Total standard direct cost per unit	$ 7.00

Irwin/McGraw-Hill
© The McGraw-Hill Companies, Inc, 1999

Material Variances

Exh. 25-10

Actual Quantity × Actual Price	Actual Quantity × Standard Price	Standard Quantity × Standard Price
3,600 yd. × $1.05 per yd.	3,600 yds. × $1.00 per yd.	3,500 yds. × $1.00 per yd.
$3,780	$3,600	$3,500

Price variance $180 unfavorable

Quantity variance $100 unfavorable

Irwin/McGraw-Hill
© The McGraw-Hill Companies, Inc, 1999

Responsibility for Material Variances

I am not responsible for this unfavorable material quantity variance.

You purchased cheap material, so my people had to use more of it.

You used too much material because of poorly trained workers and poorly maintained equipment.

Also, your poor scheduling sometimes requires me to rush order material at a higher price, causing unfavorable price variances.

Labor Variances

Actual Hours × Actual Rate	Actual Hours × Standard Rate	Standard Hours × Standard Rate

Rate Variance (Actual Hours × Actual Rate vs. Actual Hours × Standard Rate)

Efficiency Variance (Actual Hours × Standard Rate vs. Standard Hours × Standard Rate)

AH(AR - SR)	SR(AH - SH)
AH = Actual Hours	SR = Standard Rate
AR = Actual Rate	SH = Standard Hours

Labor Variances

During May, G-Max produced 3,500 hats working 3,400 hours. G-Max paid an average of $6.30 per hour for the hours worked.
Compute the labor rate and efficiency variances.

Direct materials (1 yd. per unit at $1 per yd.)	$ 1.00
Direct labor (1 hr. per unit at $6 per hr.)	6.00
Total standard direct cost per unit	$ 7.00

Labor Variances

Exh. 25-11

Actual Hours × Actual Rate	Actual Hours × Standard Rate	Standard Hours × Standard Rate
3,400 hours × $6.30 per hour	3,400 hours × $6.00 per hour	3,500 hours × $6.00 per hour
$21,420	$20,400	$21,000

Rate variance $1,020 unfavorable

Efficiency variance $600 favorable

Labor Variances

High skill, high rate

Using highly paid skilled workers to perform unskilled tasks results in an unfavorable rate variance.

Low skill, low rate

Production managers who make work assignments are generally responsible for rate variances.

Labor Variances

Unfavorable Efficiency Variance

- **Poorly trained workers**
- **Poor quality materials**
- **Poor supervision of workers**
- **Poorly maintained equipment**

Responsibility for Labor Variances

Responsibility for Labor Variances

Standard Overhead Costs

Recall that overhead costs are assigned to products and services using a predetermined overhead rate (POHR):

Assigned Overhead = POHR × Standard Activity

$$\textbf{POHR} = \frac{\textbf{Estimated total overhead costs}}{\textbf{Estimated activity}}$$

Establishing Overhead Standards

Contains a fixed overhead rate which declines as activity level increases.

Contains a variable unit rate which stays constant at all levels of activity.

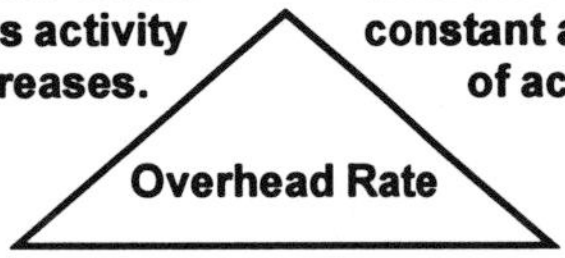

Function of activity level chosen to determine rate.

Establishing Overhead Standards

Flexible budgets, showing budgeted amount of overhead for various levels of activity, are used to analyze overhead costs.

G-Max's flexible budget for overhead

Flexible Overhead Budget

Exh. 25-12

G-Max
Overhead Costs Scenarios
For the Month Ended May 31, 1999

	Variable Amount per Unit	Total Fixed Cost	Different Production Levels (Percent of Monthly Capacity)			
			70%	80%	90%	100%
Production in units			3,500	4,000	4,500	5,000
Total variable costs	$ 1.00		$3,500	$4,000	$4,500	$5,000
Total fixed costs		$4,000	4,000	4,000	4,000	4,000
Total factory overhead			$7,500	$8,000	$8,500	$9,000
Standard direct labor hours			3,500	4,000	4,500	5,000
POHR per direct labor hour			$ 2.14	$ 2.00	$ 1.89	$ 1.80

G-Max predicted an 80 percent activity level

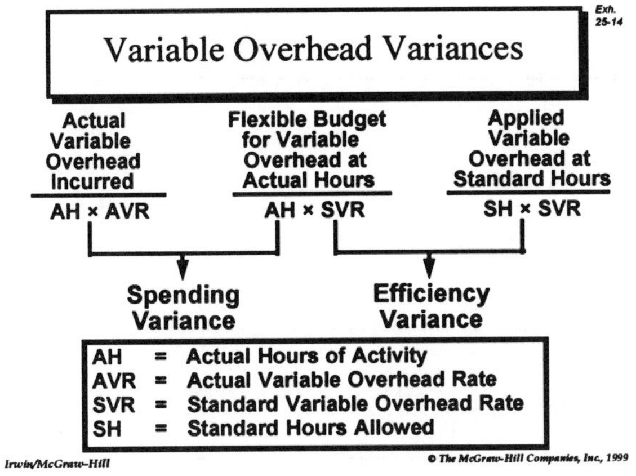
Exh. 25-14
Variable Overhead Variances
Actual Variable Overhead Incurred
AH × AVR
Flexible Budget for Variable Overhead at Actual Hours
AH × SVR
Applied Variable Overhead at Standard Hours
SH × SVR
Spending Variance
Efficiency Variance
AH = Actual Hours of Activity
AVR = Actual Variable Overhead Rate
SVR = Standard Variable Overhead Rate
SH = Standard Hours Allowed
Irwin/McGraw-Hill
© The McGraw-Hill Companies, Inc, 1999

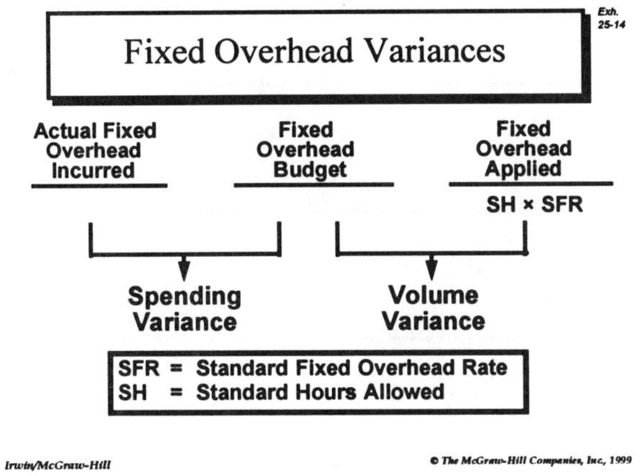
Exh. 25-14
Fixed Overhead Variances
Actual Fixed Overhead Incurred
Fixed Overhead Budget
Fixed Overhead Applied
SH × SFR
Spending Variance
Volume Variance
SFR = Standard Fixed Overhead Rate
SH = Standard Hours Allowed
Irwin/McGraw-Hill
© The McGraw-Hill Companies, Inc, 1999

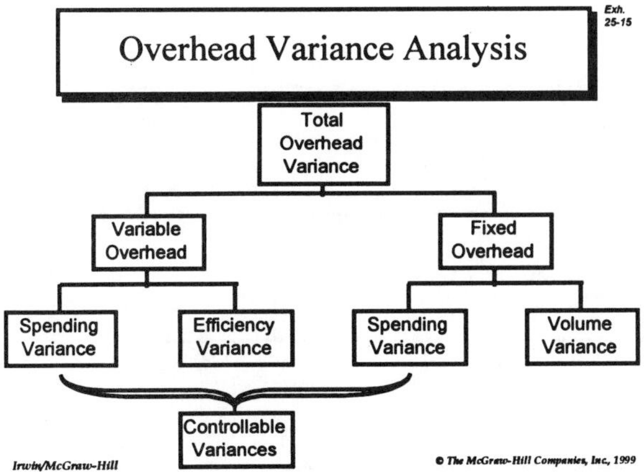
Exh. 25-15
Overhead Variance Analysis
Total Overhead Variance
Variable Overhead
Fixed Overhead
Spending Variance
Efficiency Variance
Spending Variance
Volume Variance
Controllable Variances
Irwin/McGraw-Hill
© The McGraw-Hill Companies, Inc, 1999

Computing Overhead Variances

During May, G-Max produced 3,500 hats working 3,400 hours. G-Max budgeted for 4,000 hats (80%). Actual variable overhead was $3,650 and actual fixed overhead was $4,000. Compute the variable overhead spending and efficiency variances and the fixed overhead spending and volume variances.

Computing Variable Overhead Variances

Exh. 25-16

Actual Variable Overhead Incurred	Flexible Budget for Variable Overhead at Actual Hours	Applied Variable Overhead at Standard Hours
	3,400 hours × $1.00 per hour	3,500 hours × $1.00 per hour
$3,650	$3,400	$3,500

Spending variance $250 unfavorable (between $3,650 and $3,400)

Efficiency variance $100 unfavorable (between $3,400 and $3,500)

Variable Overhead Variances

Spending Variance

Results from paying more or less than expected for overhead items and from excessive usage of overhead items.

Efficiency Variance

A function of the selected cost driver.

It does not reflect overhead control.

Computing Fixed Overhead Variances

Exh. 25-17

Actual Fixed Overhead Incurred	Fixed Overhead Budget	Fixed Overhead Applied
		3,500 hours × $1.00 per hour
$4,000	$4,000	$3,500

Spending variance $0 (between $4,000 incurred and $4,000 budget)

Volume variance $500 unfavorable (between $4,000 budget and $3,500 applied)

Fixed Overhead Variances

Spending Variance

Results from paying more or less than expected for fixed overhead items.

Volume Variance

Results from the inability to operate at the activity planned for the period.

Has no significance for cost control.

Volume Variance

Exh. 25-18

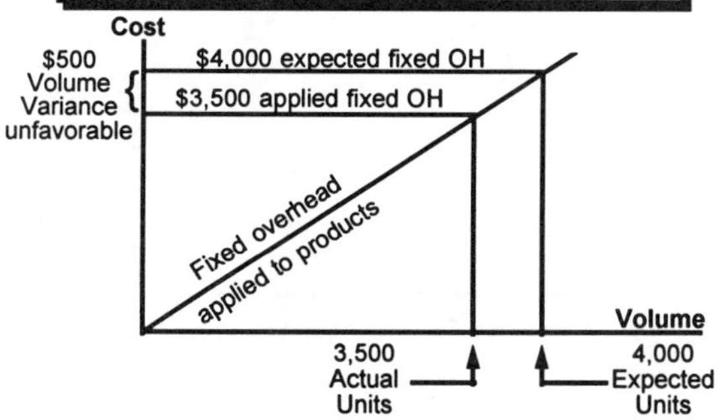

Standard Costs for Control

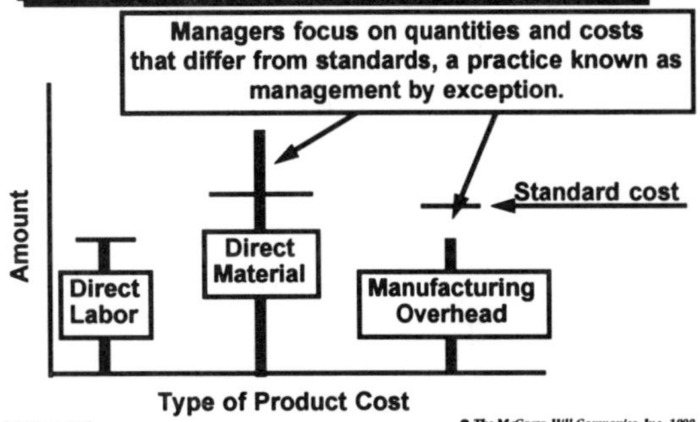

Revenue Variances

A similar analysis can be applied to revenue variances. We will use two additional G-Max products, golf balls and golf clubs, to illustrate.

	Budgeted	Actual
Sales of golf balls (units)	1,000	1,100
Sales price per golf ball	$ 10.00	$ 10.50
Sales of golf clubs (units)	150	140
Sales price per golf club	$ 200.00	$ 190.00

Computing Revenue Variances

Exh. 25-20

	Actual	Flexible Budget	Fixed Budget
Sales of golf balls (units)	1,100	1,100	1,000
Sales revenue (golf balls)	$ 11,550	$ 11,000	$ 10,000

$550 F Price Variance — $1,000 F Volume Variance

	Actual	Flexible Budget	Fixed Budget
Sales of golf clubs (units)	140	140	150
Sales revenue (golf clubs)	$ 26,600	$ 28,000	$ 30,000

$1,400 U Price Variance — $2,000 U Volume Variance

26 CHAPTER Capital Budgeting and Managerial Decisions

Capital Budgeting

❶ Outcome is uncertain.

❷ Large amounts of money are usually involved.

Capital budgeting: Analyzing alternative long-term investments and deciding which assets to acquire or sell.

❸ Investment involves a long-term commitment.

❹ Decision may be difficult or impossible to reverse.

Payback Period

Exh. 26-2

The payback period of an investment is the time expected to recover the initial investment amount.

$$\text{Payback period} = \frac{\text{Cost of Investment}}{\text{Annual Net Cash Flow}}$$

Managers prefer investing in projects with shorter payback periods.

Payback Period – Equal Cash Flows

FasTrac is considering buying a new machine that will be used in its manufacturing operations. The machine costs $16,000 and is expected to produce annual net cash flows of $4,100. The machine is expected to have an 8-year useful life with no salvage value.

Calculate the payback period.

$$\text{Payback period} = \frac{\text{Cost of Investment}}{\text{Annual Net Cash Flow}}$$

Payback Period – Unequal Cash Flows

In the previous example, we assumed that the increase in cash flows would be the same each year. Now, let's look at an example where the cash flows vary each year.

Payback Period – Unequal Cash Flows

Exh. 26-3

FasTrac wants to install a machine that costs $16,000 and has an 8-year useful life with zero salvage value. Annual net cash flows are:

Year	Annual Net Cash Flows	Cumulative Net Cash Flows
0	$ (16,000)	$ (16,000)
1	3,000	(13,000)
2	4,000	(9,000)
3	4,000	(5,000)
4	4,000	(1,000)
5	5,000	4,000
6	3,000	7,000
7	2,000	9,000
8	2,000	11,000

Payback Period – Unequal Cash Flows

Exh. 26-3

We recover the $16,000 purchase price between years 4 and 5, about 4.2 years for the payback period.

Year	Annual Net Cash Flows	Cumulative Net Cash Flows
0	$ (16,000)	$ (16,000)
1	3,000	(13,000)
2	4,000	(9,000)
3	4,000	(5,000)
4	4,000	(1,000)
4.2		
5	5,000	4,000
6	3,000	7,000
7	2,000	9,000
8	2,000	11,000

Using the Payback Period

Unacceptable for projects with long lives where time value of money effects are major.

Ignores the time value of money.

Ignores cash flows after the payback period.

Using the Payback Period

Consider two projects, each with a five-year life and each costing $6,000.

Year	Project One Net Cash Inflows	Project Two Net Cash Inflows
1	$ 2,000	$ 1,000
2	2,000	1,000
3	2,000	1,000
4	2,000	1,000
5	2,000	1,000,000

Would you invest in Project One just because it has a shorter payback period?

Exh. 26-5,6

Accounting Rate of Return

The accounting rate of return focuses on annual income instead of cash flows.

$$\text{Accounting rate of return} = \frac{\text{Annual after-tax net income}}{\text{Annual average investment}}$$

Annual average investment $= \dfrac{\text{Beginning book value + Ending book value}}{2}$

Exh. 26-5,6

Accounting Rate of Return

Reconsider the $16,000 investment being considered by FasTrac. The annual after-tax net income is $2,100. Compute the accounting rate of return.

$$\text{Accounting rate of return} = \frac{\text{Annual after-tax net income}}{\text{Annual average investment}}$$

Annual average investment $= \dfrac{\text{Beginning book value + Ending book value}}{2}$

Using Accounting Rate of Return

- Depreciation may be calculated several ways.
- Income may vary from year to year.
- Time value of money is ignored.

Net Present Value

Now let's look at a capital budgeting model that considers the time value of cash flows.

Net Present Value

❶ Discount the future net cash flows from the investment at the required rate of return

❷ Subtract the initial amount invested from sum of the discounted cash flows.

FasTrac is considering the purchase of a conveyor costing $16,000 with an 8-year useful life with zero salvage value that promises annual net cash flows of $4,100. FasTrac requires a 12 percent compounded annual return on its investments.

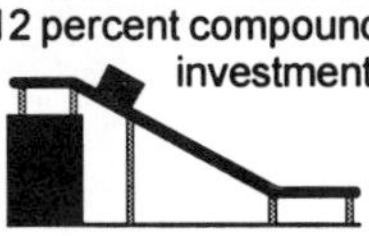

Net Present Value with Equal Cash Flows

Exh. 26-7

Year	Annual Net Cash Flows	Present Value of $1 Factor	Present Value of Cash Flows
1	$ 4,100	0.8929	$ 3,661
2	4,100	0.7972	3,269
3	4,100	0.7118	2,918
4	4,100	0.6355	2,606
5	4,100	0.5674	2,326
6	4,100	0.5066	2,077
7	4,100	0.4523	1,854
8	4,100	0.4039	1,656
Total	$ 32,800		$ 20,367
Amount to be invested			(16,000)
Net present value of investment			$ 4,367

Using Net Present Value

General decision rule . . .

If the Net Present Value is . . .	Then the Project is . . .
Positive . . .	Acceptable, since it promises a return greater than the required rate of return.
Zero . . .	Acceptable, since it promises a return equal to the required rate of return.
Negative . . .	Not acceptable, since it promises a return less than the required rate of return.

Net Present Value with Unequal Cash Flows

Exh. 26-8

Year	Net Cash Flows A	Net Cash Flows B	Net Cash Flows C	Present Value of $1 Factor at 10%	PV of Net Cash Flows A	PV of Net Cash Flows B	PV of Net Cash Flows C
1	$ 5,000	$ 8,000	$ 1,000	0.9091	$ 4,546	$ 7,273	$ 909
2	5,000	5,000	5,000	0.8264	4,132	4,132	4,132
3	5,000	2,000	9,000	0.7513	3,757	1,503	6,762
Total	$15,000	$15,000	$15,000		$12,435	$ 12,908	$ 11,803
Amount invested					(12,000)	(12,000)	(12,000)
Net Present Value					$ 435	$ 908	$ (197)

Although all projects require the same investment and have the same total net cash flows, project B has a higher net present value because of a larger net cash flow in year 1.

Internal Rate of Return

The interest rate that makes . . .

❶ **Present value of cash inflows = Present value of cash outflows**

❷ The net present value equal zero.

Exh. 26-9

Computing Internal Rate of Return

Projects with equal annual cash flows

Project life = 3 years
Initial cost = $12,000
Annual net cash inflows = $5,000
Determine the IRR for this project.

1. **Compute present value factor.**

2. **Using present value of annuity table . . .**

Exh. 26-9

Computing Internal Rate of Return

1. Determine the present value factor.

   $12,000 ÷ $5,000 per year = 2.4000

2. Using present value of annuity table . . .

IRR is approximately 12%.

IRR is the interest rate of the column in which the present value factor is found.

Periods	10%	12%	14%
1	0.90909	[illegible]	0.87719
2	1.73554	[illegible]	1.64666
3	[illegible]	2.40183	2.32163
4	3.16987	[illegible]	2.91371
5	3.79079	3.60478	3.43308

Internal Rate of Return – Unequal Cash Flows

If cash inflows are unequal, trial and error solution will result if present value tables are used.

Sophisticated business calculators and electronic spreadsheets can be used to easily solve these problems.

Using Internal Rate of Return

Internal Rate of Return

- Compare the internal rate of return on a project to a predetermined hurdle rate (cost of capital).
- To be acceptable, a project's rate of return cannot be less than the cost of capital.

Comparing Methods

Exh. 26-10

	Payback period	Accounting rate of return	Net present value	Internal rate of return
Basis of measurement	Cash flows	Accrual income	Cash flows Profitability	Cash flows Profitability
Measure expressed as	Number of years	Percent	Dollar Amount	Percent
Strengths	Easy to Understand Allows comparison across projects	Easy to Understand Allows comparison across projects	Considers time value of money Accommodates different risk levels over a project's life	Considers time value of money Allows comparisons of dissimilar projects
Limitations	Doesn't consider time value of money Doesn't consider cash flows after payback period	Doesn't consider time value of money Doesn't give annual rates over the life of a project	Difficult to compare dissimilar projects	Doesn't reflect varying risk levels over the project's life

Decision Making

Decision making involves five steps:

❶ Define the problem.
❷ Identify alternatives.
❸ Collect relevant information on alternatives.
❹ Select the preferred alternative.
❺ Analyze decisions made.

Relevant Costs

- Costs that are applicable to a particular decision.
- Costs that should have a bearing on which alternative a manager selects.
- Costs that are avoidable.
- Future costs that differ between alternatives.

Classification by Relevance: Sunk Costs

All costs incurred in the past that cannot be changed by any decision made now or in the future.

Sunk costs should not be considered in decisions.

Example: You bought an automobile that cost $10,000 two years ago. The $10,000 cost is sunk because whether you drive it, park it, trade it, or sell it, you cannot change the $10,000 cost.

Classification by Relevance: Out-of-Pocket Costs

Future outlays of cash associated with a particular decision.

Example: Considering the decision to take a vacation or stay at home, you will only have travel costs (out-of-pocket costs) if you choose a vacation.

Classification by Relevance: Opportunity Costs

The potential benefit that is given up when one alternative is selected over another.

- Example: If you were not attending college, you could be earning $15,000 per year. Your opportunity cost of attending college for one year is $15,000.

Irwin/McGraw-Hill

Accepting Additional Business

The decision to accept additional business should be based on incremental costs and incremental revenues.

Incremental amounts are those that occur if the company decides to accept the new business.

Irwin/McGraw-Hill

Accepting Additional Business

Exh. 26-12

FasTrac currently sells 100,000 units of its product. The company has revenue and costs as shown below:

	Per Unit	Total
Sales	$ 10.00	$ 1,000,000
Direct materials	3.50	350,000
Direct labor	2.20	220,000
Factory overhead	1.10	110,000
Selling expenses	1.40	140,000
Administrative expenses	0.80	80,000
Total expenses	$ 9.00	$ 900,000
Operating income	$ 1.00	$ 100,000

Irwin/McGraw-Hill

Accepting Additional Business

FasTrac is approached by an overseas company that offers to purchase 10,000 units at $8.50 per unit.

If FasTrac accepts the offer, total factory overhead will increase by $5,000; total selling expenses will increase by $2,000; and total administrative expenses will increase by $1,000.

Should FasTrac accept the offer?

Accepting Additional Business

First let's look at incorrect reasoning that leads to an incorrect decision.

Exh. 26-14

Accepting Additional Business

	Current Business	Additional Business	Combined
Sales	$ 1,000,000	$ 85,000	$ 1,085,000
Direct materials	$ 350,000	$ 35,000	$ 385,000
Direct labor	220,000	22,000	242,000
Factory overhead	110,000	5,000	115,000
Selling expenses	140,000	2,000	142,000
Admin. expenses	80,000	1,000	81,000
Total expenses	$ 900,000	$ 65,000	$ 965,000
Operating income	$ 100,000	$ 20,000	$ 120,000

This analysis leads to the correct decision.

Make or Buy Decisions

- Incremental costs also are important in the decision to make a product or purchase it from a supplier.
- The cost to produce an item must include (1) direct materials, (2) direct labor and (3) incremental overhead.
- We should not use the predetermined overhead rate to determine product cost.

Make or Buy Decisions

FasTrac currently makes part #417, assigning overhead at 100 percent of direct labor cost, with the following unit cost:

Cost to Make Part #417

	Make
Direct materials	$0.45
Direct labor	0.50
Factory overhead	0.50
Total cost to make	$1.45

Exh. 26-15

Make or Buy Decisions

FasTrac can buy part #417 from a supplier for $1.20. How much overhead do we have to eliminate before we can continue to make this part?

Make vs. Buy Analysis

	Make	Buy
Direct materials	$0.45	—
Direct labor	0.50	—
Factory overhead	?	—
Purchase price	—	$1.20
Total incremental costs	?	$1.20

Scrap or Rework Defects

Costs incurred in manufacturing units of product that do not meet quality standards are sunk costs and cannot be recovered.

As long as rework costs are recovered through sale of the product, and rework does not interfere with normal production, we should rework rather than scrap.

Scrap or Rework Defects

FasTrac has 10,000 defective units that cost $1.00 each to make. The units can be scrapped now for $.40 each or reworked at an additional cost of $.80 per unit.

If reworked, the units can be sold for the normal selling price of $1.50 each. Reworking the defective units will prevent the production of 10,000 new units that would also sell for $1.50.

Should FasTrac scrap or rework?

Exh. 26-16

Scrap or Rework Defects

FasTrac should scrap the units now.

	Scrap Now	Rework
Sale of Defects	$ 4,000	$ 15,000
Less rework costs	-	(8,000)
Less opportunity cost	-	(5,000)
Net return	$ 4,000	2,000

If FasTrac fails to include the opportunity cost, the rework option would show a return of $7,000, mistakenly making rework appear more favorable.

Sell or Process Further

- Businesses are often faced with the decision to sell partially completed products or to process them to completion.
- As a general rule, we process further only if incremental revenues exceed incremental costs.

Sell or Process Further

FasTrac has 40,000 units of partially finished product Q. Processing costs to date are $30,000. The 40,000 unfinished units can be sold as is for $50,000 or they can be processed further to produce finished products X, Y, and Z. The additional processing will cost $80,000 and result in the following revenues:

Continue

Exh. 26-17

Sell or Process Further

Product	Price	Units	Revenue
X	$ 4.00	10,000	$ 40,000
Y	6.00	22,000	132,000
Z	8.00	6,000	48,000
Spoilage	-	2,000	-
Total		40,000	$ 220,000

Should FasTrac sell product Q or continue processing into products X, Y, and Z?

Selecting Sales Mix

- When a company sells a variety of products, some are likely to be more profitable than others.
- To make an informed decision, management must consider . . .
  - The contribution margin of each product,
  - The facilities required to produce each product and any constraints on the facilities, and
  - The demand for each product.

Selecting Sales Mix

Consider the following data for two products made and sold by FasTrac.

Per unit amounts	Product A	Product B
Selling price	$ 5.00	$ 7.50
Variable costs	3.50	5.50
Contribution margin	$ 1.50	$ 2.00

If each product requires the same time to make, and the demand is unlimited, FasTrac should produce only product B.

Exh. 26-19

Selecting Sales Mix

Consider the following data for two products made and sold by FasTrac.

Per unit amounts	Product A	Product B
Selling price	$ 5.00	$ 7.50
Variable costs	3.50	5.50
Contribution margin	$ 1.50	$ 2.00
Machine hours required to produce one unit	1.0	2.0
Contribution per machine hour	$ 1.50	$ 1.00

Consider this additional information.

Exh. 26-19

Selecting Sales Mix

Consider the following data for two products ... d by FasTrac.

Product B has a greater contribution margin than Product A, but it requires more machine hours per unit to produce.

	Product A	Product B
	$ 5.00	$ 7.50
	3.50	5.50
Contribution margin	$ 1.50	$ 2.00
Machine hours required to produce one unit	1.0	2.0
Contribution per machine hour	$ 1.50	$ 1.00

With unlimited demand for A and B, produce as many units of A as possible since A provides more dollars per hour worked.

Eliminating a Segment

A segment is a candidate for elimination if its revenues are less than its avoidable expenses.

FasTrac is considering eliminating its Treadmill Division because total expenses of $48,300 are greater than its sales of $47,800.

Continue

Exh. 26-20

Analysis of Divisional Operating Expenses

	Total Expenses	Avoidable Expenses	Unavoidable Expenses
Cost of goods sold	$ 30,200	$ 30,200	
Direct expenses:			
Salaries	7,900	7,900	
Equipment depreciation	200		$ 200
Indirect expenses:			
Rent and utilities	3,150		3,150
Advertising	200	200	
Insurance	400	300	100
Service department costs:			
Departmental office	3,060	2,200	860
Purchasing	3,190	1,000	2,190
Total	$ 48,300	$ 41,800	$ 6,500

Eliminating a Segment

Sales	$ 47,800
Avoidable expenses	41,800
Decrease in income	$ 6,000

Qualitative Factors in Decisions

Qualitative factors are involved in most all managerial decisions. For example:

- **Quality.**
- **Delivery schedule.**
- **Supplier reputation.**
- **Employee morale.**
- **Customer opinions.**

GO FOR IT!

Break-Even Time

Break-even time incorporates time value of money into the payback period method of evaluating capital investments.